The
TEACHER'S
Guide to
Restorative Classroom
Discipline

The
TEACHER'S
Guide to
Restorative Classroom Discipline

Luanna H. Meyer
Ian M. Evans

CORWIN

A SAGE Company.

CORWIN
A SAGE Company

FOR INFORMATION:

Corwin
A SAGE Company
2455 Teller Road
Thousand Oaks, California 91320
(800) 233-9936
www.corwin.com

SAGE Publications Ltd.
1 Oliver's Yard
55 City Road
London EC1Y 1SP
United Kingdom

SAGE Publications India Pvt. Ltd.
B 1/I 1 Mohan Cooperative Industrial Area
Mathura Road, New Delhi 110 044
India

SAGE Publications Asia-Pacific Pte. Ltd.
3 Church Street
#10-04 Samsung Hub
Singapore 049483

Acquisitions Editor: Jessica Allan
Associate Editor: Allison Scott
Editorial Assistant: Lisa Whitney
Production Editor: Amy Schroller
Copy Editor: Janet Ford
Typesetter: C&M Digitals (P) Ltd.
Proofreader: Christine Dahlin
Indexer: Judy Hunt
Cover Designer: Rose Storey
Graphic Designer: Karine Hovsepian
Permissions Editor: Karen Ehrmann

Printed in the United States of America

Library of Congress Cataloging-in-Publication Data

Meyer, Luanna H.
The teacher's guide to restorative classroom discipline/Luanna H. Meyer, Ian M. Evans.

p. cm.

Includes bibliographical references and index.

ISBN 978-1-4129-9861-1 (pbk. : alk. paper)
1. Classroom management. 2. School discipline.
3. Problem children—Behavior modification.
I. Evans, Ian M., 1944- II. Title.

LB3013.M475 2012
371.102′4—dc23   2012013396

This book is printed on acid-free paper.

Certified Chain of Custody
SUSTAINABLE   Promoting Sustainable Forestry
FORESTRY   www.sfiprogram.org
INITIATIVE   SFI-01268

SFI label applies to text stock

12 13 14 15 16 10 9 8 7 6 5 4 3 2 1

Contents

List of Tables and Figures   xi

Acknowledgments   xiii

About the Authors   xv

Introduction to the Guide   **1**
    Learning Outcomes   2

SECTION I. SETTING THE CONTEXT

Chapter 1: Restorative Classroom Discipline   **5**
    Key Characteristics of Classrooms That
       Support Restorative Practices   5
    The Importance of Classroom Climate   6
    Planning and Establishing Restorative Practices   7
       Restorative Practices as Classroom Ethos   8
       Restorative Practices as Prevention and Intervention   9
       Restorative Classroom Discipline Planning   10
    Summary   11

**Chapter 2: Behavior Expectations
for Schools and Classrooms**   **13**
    What Are Schoolwide Behavior Expectations?   14
       Your Role in Developing the School's
          Behavior Expectations   16
       Developing Behavior Expectations for
          Your Classroom   17
    Summary   21

Chapter 3: Home-School and Community Relationships   **23**
    Establishing Positive Home-School Relationships   23
       Approaches to Home-School Interactions   24
    Culture, Context, and Intercultural Competence   25

Cultural Mismatches Between Home and School 26
Culturally Competent Teachers 27
Home-School Partnerships 28
Home-School Relationships and Behavioral Challenges 29
Strategies to Build Home-School Partnerships 31
Summary 34

SECTION II. PUTTING THE MODEL IN PLACE

Chapter 4: Classroom Climate and Cultural Responsiveness 37
Establishing a Warm Classroom Climate 37
Secondary Classrooms 41
Identifying and reducing risk for harm 41
Classwide strategies 42
An example: Abbas 42
Elementary Classrooms 44
An example: Disruption in third grade 46
School Climate as the Context for
Classroom Climate 46
Teaching Styles 48
Culturally Responsive Relationships 50
Culturally Responsive Authentic Caring 51
Culturally Responsive Pedagogies 52
Summary 54

Chapter 5: School and Classroom Support Structures 55
Community and Peer Support in Classrooms 55
Cooperative Learning Structures 57
Constructing Peer Support Networks 59
Ongoing Group Problem-Solving Processes 64
Collaborative Problem Solving 65
Bullying 69
Identifying Bullying 70
Cyberbullying 70
Preventing and Intervening With Bullying 72
Restorative Classroom Discipline Structures and Processes 73
Restorative Curricula 73
Mediation 76
Peer mediation 77
Shuttle mediation 78
Mentoring 78
Restorative Classroom Conferencing 79
Summary 81

Chapter 6: Interventions for Individual Students—
Child-Focused Planning   83
  Secondary and Tertiary Prevention and Intervention   84
  Implications: Applying General Principles   86
    A High School Example: Jayla   87
  Avoiding Deficit Discussions About Children   87
  Understanding Barriers to Change   90
  Restorative Practices That Are Culturally Responsive   91
    An Elementary School Example: Nikotemo   91
  Incorporating Mediator Perspectives and Capabilities   93
  Introducing the Four-Component Intervention Model   97
  Summary   98

Chapter 7: Interventions for Individual
Students—Principles in Practice   99
  Prevent—Altering Antecedent Settings and Events   100
    Ecological Change   100
    Prevention   101
  Educate—Teaching Positive Replacement Skills   102
    Replacement Skills Should Serve the Same Function   103
    Appropriate Alternatives   104
  Restore—Consequences, Not Retribution   106
    Natural Consequences   106
    Safety Considerations   107
  Think—Teaching New Understandings and Emotional Skills   108
    Cognitive and Emotional Distortions   109
  Examples of the Four-Component Model in Action   110
    An Elementary School Student Example: Justin   110
      Prevent   111
      Educate   112
      Restore   114
      Think   114
    A Middle School Student Example: Dilbert   115
      Prevent   117
      Educate   117
      Restore   117
      Think   117
    A High School Student Example: Fernanda   118
      Prevent   120
      Educate   121
      Restore   122
      Think   122
  Summary   124

Chapter 8: Reflecting Schoolwide
Policy in Teacher Practice   **125**

    Making Decisions About Behavior
      and Its Consequences   125
    Recording Behavioral Incidents Objectively   128
      Office Discipline Referral (ODR)   128
      What to Include in Incident Reports for ODRs   129
    Restorative Conferencing at School Level   133
      When Is a Restorative Conference Needed?   133
      What Should Be the Goal of a Restorative Conference?   134
      Who Should Facilitate the Restorative Conference?   134
      Administrative Support for Restorative Conferences   135
    In-School Suspension   135
      Key Components of In-School Suspension   138
    Suicide Prevention, Intervention, and Postvention   143
      Responding to Risk for Student Suicide   143
      What to Do in the Classroom   145
      Teacher Self-Assessment   147
    Threat Assessment   149
    Managing Conflict and Breaking Up Fights   151
      Supportive Demands   153
      Assertive Demands   155
    A Standard Response Protocol (SRP) for School Safety   157
    Summary   159

SECTION III: EVALUATING
EFFECTIVENESS AND UPDATING PRACTICE

Chapter 9: User-Friendly Evaluation
Tools and Approaches   **163**

    Meaningful Outcomes for Students and Schools   163
      Overall Developmental Measures   164
      Meaningful Behavior Change   165
    User-Friendly Data Collection   166
    Data Collection for Problem Behavior   167
      Self-Monitoring   167
      Daily Log   168
      Daily and Weekly Schedules   168
      Incident Records   171
    Summary   171

Chapter 10: Professional Development Needs Assessment   **175**
    The Need for Ongoing Professional Development   175
    The PD Needs Assessment Tool for Restorative Discipline   177

References   **183**
Index   **191**

List of Tables and Figures

Tables

Table 1. Behavior Expectations at Jarrett Middle School   15

Table 2. Disproportionality in Suspensions   39

Table 3. Criteria for Constructing Peer Support Networks   61

Table 4. An Example of Collaborative Problem Solving in an Elementary Classroom   68

Table 5. Rethinking Negative Conversations about Children With Challenging Behavior   88

Table 6. Incident Report for Office Discipline Referrals   130

Table 7. Minor versus Major Behavior Problems in Schools   132

Table 8. The Home-School, In-School Suspension Contract   140

Table 9. Forms for In-School Suspension Reflections   141

Table 10. Test Your Knowledge About What to Do for Suicide-Related Incidents   147

Figures

Figure 1. Student Interest Inventory for Elementary School   62

Figure 2. Student Interest Inventory for Middle and High School   62

Figure 3. Group Lesson in Art for First-Grade Students   64

Figure 4. Mediator Worksheet with Teacher or
          Parent as Mediator   95

Figure 5. Effort to Implement Scale   96

Figure 6. Sample Daily Log   169

Figure 7. Sample Student Schedule Record   170

Figure 8. Sample Incident Record   172

Acknowledgments

Corwin gratefully acknowledges the contributions of the following reviewers:

Carol S. Cash

Assistant Clinical Professor

Virginia Tech

School of Education

Richmond, VA

Lyman Goding

Principal (Retired)

Plymouth Community Intermediate School

Sandwich, MA

Steve Knobl

High School Principal

Pasco County Schools

Gulf High School

New Port Richey, FL

Neil MacNeill

Principal

Ellenbrook Primary School

Ellenbrook, Western Australia

Natalie Marston
Principal
Anne Arundel County Public Schools
Central Special Education Center
Edgewater, MD

Jadi K. Miller
Principal
Elliott Elementary School
Lincoln, NE

Mary Reeve
Director, Special Education and Gifted Services
Gallup McKinley County Schools
Gallup, NM

About the Authors

 **Luanna H. Meyer** is professor of education (research) and director of the Jessie Hetherington Center for Educational Research at Victoria University in New Zealand. She is also professor emerita at Syracuse University in the United States and adjunct professor at Griffith University in Australia. Since receiving her PhD from Indiana University, she held faculty positions at the University of Hawai'i, the University of Minnesota, Syracuse University, and Massey University prior to her current position. While at Syracuse University, she cofounded the Inclusive Elementary and Special Education Teacher Education Program and coordinated the doctoral program in special education. She also led numerous federally funded research and development projects, including a five-year research institute on the social relationships of children and youth with diverse abilities and the 10-year New York Partnership for Statewide Systems Change.

Throughout her career as a teacher educator and educational researcher, Luanna has been committed to developing practical, evidence-based approaches that can be implemented in real-life, typical situations and settings. She works closely with school leaders, teachers, and behavior specialists toward achieving inclusive schools where all children and youth belong and feel valued. Her contributions to the development of positive approaches to behavior problems are acknowledged by her appointment to the *Technical Review Committee on Behavior for the National Center for Students with Disabilities Who Require Intensive Interventions* led by the American Institutes for Research. She was among the first to demonstrate that even the most severe behavior can be managed with positive approaches and this premise is supported by her published research conducted in typical settings with children with severe behavior disorders, autism, and other disabilities. In New Zealand, her current federally funded projects include research on culturally responsive behavioral intervention in schools; culturally responsive pedagogies for teachers; effective school-based behavioral intervention practices; and the impact of assessment design on student motivation and achievement in secondary schools across the curriculum. A major focus of this work is on effective policy and practice to meet the needs of an increasingly diverse community in regular education schools.

Luanna has been invited to speak about her work in eight countries and 30 U.S. states, and she has published more than 120 journal articles and book chapters. Her 12 books include *Making Friends: The Influences of Culture and Development; Critical Issues in the Lives of People with Severe Disabilities; Behavioral Intervention: Principles, Models, and Practices; The Syracuse Community-Referenced Curriculum Guide; Nonaversive Intervention for Behavior Problems: A Manual for Home and Community;* and *An Educative Approach to Behavior Problems: A Practical Decision Model.*

Just as important, Luanna is a proud parent and grandparent.

 **Ian M. Evans** is professor of psychology at Massey University in New Zealand. After his PhD at the University of London's Institute of Psychiatry, he taught behavior assessment and therapy for many years at the University of Hawai'i while also serving as consultant psychologist to specialized programs for children and adults with very complex developmental needs. He founded the Hawai'i Association for Autistic Children and was appointed commissioner on the Governor's State Planning and Advisory Council for Developmental Disabilities. At this time, funded by a federal research grant on children's challenging behavior, he and Luanna Meyer began their collaborative work in the public schools across the state. After becoming director of clinical psychology training at SUNY-Binghamton, Ian continued his focus on disabilities in addition to leading the Binghamton Liberty Partnership Project. This intervention research was funded by state and federal grants to work with elementary schools to prevent school dropout, using a home-visitor model to enhance teacher-parent communication. His book *Staying in School: Partnerships for Educational Change* reports this work and that of colleagues across New York State evaluating initiatives in regular education to support children,

families, and the schools. Since moving to New Zealand in 1995, he has been professor, clinical program director, and department head at the University of Waikato and then Massey University. His most recent work is teacher-focused research to enhance the emotional atmosphere in elementary school classrooms resulting in a book and several journal articles. His long-standing commitment to children with autism and their families has been recognized with honors, including being named life member of the advocacy group Parent-to-Parent. He is a fellow of the American Psychological Association and a fellow of the Royal Society of New Zealand.

His other interests include photography, antiques of the Arts and Crafts period, taking long nonstrenuous walks, wine tasting, and watching his grandchildren develop.

Introduction
to the Guide

This guide for teachers is one of three guides comprising a comprehensive approach to restorative discipline for elementary, middle, and high schools. The guide is:

- *Evidence-based*—drawing on the latest research in education and psychology on effective strategies for educative discipline in classrooms.
- *Inclusive*—classroom strategies that accommodate different behavior support needs to ensure emotionally safe and secure learning environments that do not exclude children and youth.
- *Restorative*—incorporating approaches that focus on making things right, not on retribution for things that have gone wrong.
- *Practical*— based on the kinds of resources and personnel generally available to teachers, disciplinary frameworks and intervention approaches that are do-able in typical elementary, middle, and high school classrooms.
- *Contextual*—socially valid principles and practices that fit comfortably in regular classrooms and that reflect community values about how children and youth should be treated.
- *Culturally responsive*—educationally meaningful guidelines for culturally responsive policy and practice in linguistically and culturally diverse communities.
- *User-friendly*—presented in a succinct format respectful of the multiple responsibilities, busy schedules, and existing capabilities of teachers with theoretical constructs, references, and intervention descriptions directly relevant to the teacher's role in restorative schools and classrooms.

Learning Outcomes

This guide includes the information needed to ensure learning outcomes for teachers leading to:

1. *Restorative Discipline Classroom Community*—ensuring that the underlying values and driving strengths of your classroom are positive relationships, where each member of that classroom community feels a sense of belonging, is valued, and accepts responsibility for the well-being of others.

2. *Culturally Responsive Behavior Expectations for the Classroom*— under the supervision of the classroom teacher, applies to children and adults in the classroom, in common areas of the school, and during transitions.

3. *Effective Four-Component Behavioral Interventions*—based on current research relevant to schools, understanding a framework for interventions to address challenging behavior in students in a positive way.

4. *Support Teams and Networks*—backed by appropriate referrals to other child and youth services such as mental health and social welfare services, collaborating with all team members, including family members and specialist behavioral consultants working together to support students.

5. *Schoolwide Restorative Discipline*—alignment with school policy and practices, including Office Discipline Referrals, responding to incidents or threats, restorative conferencing, in-school suspension, and school safety crisis intervention.

6. *Ongoing Professional Development for Sustainability*—self-assessment of the skills and understandings needed to promote restorative discipline, culturally responsive practices, social-emotional support, and high expectations for learning and behavior.

Section I

Setting the Context

1 Restorative Classroom Discipline

This chapter describes the major features providing a foundation for a restorative discipline approach to school policies and practices that are reflected in what happens for students in classrooms and throughout the school. It provides essential information for sharing with the classroom community and focuses on the processes for planning and introducing Restorative Classroom Discipline in individual classrooms, and on building understandings and skills in restorative practices at all ages and in all school settings.

KEY CHARACTERISTICS OF CLASSROOMS THAT SUPPORT RESTORATIVE PRACTICES

What does a classroom with restorative discipline policies and practices look like? Here are some of the key characteristics of such classrooms (adapted from McCluskey et al., 2008):

- Positive classroom climate inclusive of all students, where students have a strong sense of belonging rather than being at risk for exclusion
- Students experience positive learning relationships with the teacher and with one another, feel safe, have a high regard for their class, and are given the opportunity to make things right when things go wrong
- Culturally responsive pedagogy underpins the teacher's approach to the diversity in the classroom

- The teacher focuses on students' strengths, rejects deficit explanations for failure, and takes agency for successful educational outcomes for children and youth
- Families feel welcomed by the teacher and able to visit the classroom freely, participate in activities designed for them with the teacher, regularly receive information about how their young person is doing, and are involved in supporting their child's education as appropriate, including collaborating actively to address problems
- Average daily attendance is high, all absences must be excused for valid reasons, and there is timely daily follow-up by the teacher and the school when students are absent or tardy
- Students receive support and encouragement to meet their educational and social-emotional needs, including positive classroom relationships with peers, teachers with high expectations, and established pedagogies that enable them to achieve to the best of their abilities
- Reasonable and well-understood behavior expectations for children and youth are agreed, specified, and shared within the classroom
- Restorative Classroom Discipline practices with clear definitions of behavior and consequences are in place, known to students, and communicated with families
- Ongoing back-up supports are in place, including threat assessment, crisis management, and in-school suspension to deal with serious behavior
- Restorative practices and mutual respect are the foundations for interactions within the classroom community, not retribution and punishment
- Agency is promoted with responsibility to add value to every student's achievement each year without exception or excuses attributed to background characteristics or challenges such as socioeconomic, linguistic, or environmental circumstances

THE IMPORTANCE OF CLASSROOM CLIMATE

A positive classroom climate is the foundation for restorative practices that sit alongside and support teaching and learning. Classroom climate is influenced and shaped by four major aspects of school life (Cohen, McCabe, Michelli, & Pickeral, 2009). These are:

- *Safety:* Safety encompasses physical aspects such as attitudes about violence, clearly communicated rules, everyone feeling physically safe, and teachers knowing and adhering to agreed crisis plans. At the social and emotional level for teachers and students, there is respect for individual differences, conflict resolution is taught, and the response to bullying (including cyberbullying) is explicit and fair.

- *Pedagogy:* There is a focus on the quality of instruction, including discursive teaching and active learning; social, emotional, and ethical learning; professional development and professionalism for teachers; and school management who work with teaching staff on curricula, instruction, and pastoral care issues.
- *Relationships:* Relationships in the classroom highlight respect for diversity, shared decision making, and the value of each classroom as a learning community. Teachers and students are connected to and feel good about their school.
- *Environment:* The classroom environment is clean and well maintained; adequate space is available for instructional and extracurricular activities; materials and resources are adequate; support services are available when needed; and the classroom has an inviting aesthetic quality.

The context for the teacher's guide is closely related to holistic ideas underlying the importance of a classroom climate where restorative practices protect *safety* and relationships. Children need healthy physical environments and effective pedagogical practices as a foundation for teaching and learning activities, and the effectiveness of Restorative Classroom Discipline is influenced by these qualities. Teachers cannot guarantee that physical environments are always optimal for teaching and learning, of course; some things may be beyond their reach to change such as the physical condition of a building or the qualifications of support staff. Nevertheless, teachers can work alongside their school leaders to establish restorative practices that optimize children's learning and behavior.

PLANNING AND ESTABLISHING RESTORATIVE PRACTICES

If your school attends to the kinds of school climate issues included above, you have strong support for establishing restorative practices in your classroom. This section of the guide describes how teachers can contribute to restorative practices at both the school and classroom level.

Restorative Practices as Classroom Ethos

The approach described in this guide as "Restorative Classroom Discipline" is not an add-on program for the purposes of behavior management, nor does it provide just another tool in the teacher's toolbox for use in dealing with student behavior. In fact, Restorative Classroom Discipline represents an ethos that permeates all aspects of classroom organization and relationships that children experience within and outside of the classroom. Fundamentally, restorative school practices signify a rejection of *punishment and retribution* as educational responses to challenging behavior and conflict. Punishment and retribution approaches to problem behavior and conflict typically characterize the criminal justice system in many countries, but they do not reflect educational goals that acknowledge the classroom and school as social communities and children as members of their communities who require support, not exclusion.

In contrast to retribution, the primary aim of restorative practices is the development of positive relationships and peaceful resolution of conflict for teachers and students. Restorative Classroom Discipline is not simply a behavior management system, though it includes the key elements of positive behavior management described in general terms as "educative" and "non-aversive" (Evans & Meyer, 1985; Meyer & Evans, 1989) and in specific models as "Positive Behavior Support" (Dunlap, Sailor, Horner, & Sugai, 2009; Sugai et al., 2005) and "Positive Behavior for Learning" (Savage, Lewis, & Colless, 2011). While Restorative Classroom Discipline utilizes strategies developed and validated through decades of behavior management intervention research, it differs from behavior management approaches by starting from a relationship perspective where the focus is on context, organization, and culture. It is not strictly a bottom-up approach that emphasizes descriptions of acceptable and unacceptable behavior within deficit intervention frameworks. Nor is it top-down in asserting classroom rules set by the teacher whereby violations are viewed as transgressions against rules. Instead, Restorative Classroom Discipline is people-focused, accepting that positive and supportive relationships are crucial for learning to occur in educational environments. Conflict must be addressed by making amends, or relationships will otherwise be damaged and even broken.

Restorative Classroom Discipline also goes beyond being simply a philosophy or set of principles. Restorative Classroom Discipline concurs with the societal goal that the primary purpose of schools is to *educate*. This responsibility to educate goes beyond basic skills such as literacy, numeracy, and subject knowledge: it includes education for citizenship and becoming contributing members of one's community. Thus, restorative practices are grounded in educative principles for providing all members of the school community with skills and understandings about positive social interactions and relationships that support learning and peaceful resolution of problems and conflict.

Restorative Practices as Prevention and Intervention

Restorative practices entail a comprehensive framework and strategies that have been empirically validated as effective at three levels:

- *Prevention:* Restorative practices are the foundation for a positive classroom climate that encourages and supports teaching and learning. For both teachers and students, it provides the framework for developing social and emotional competencies for achieving caring relationships and peaceful resolution of conflict. This level is sometimes referred to as Tier 1 in the literature (Campbell & Anderson, 2008).

- *Secondary intervention:* Restorative Classroom Discipline encompasses a systematic, positive, and accountable set of practices that have been demonstrated to be effective in addressing specific incidents of harmful acts or threats. These practices include more formal processes for restoration of relationships such as ongoing problem solving, and conferencing and mediation to repair harm and prevent future incidents. Secondary intervention approaches are also designed to address the needs of children who typically require individualized support services on at least a temporary basis at different times in their school careers (generally considered to be approximately 15 percent of the school population), but these services are fit within the overall ethos of Restorative Classroom Discipline and not as something added or different. This level parallels what is referred to as Tier 2 in the literature (Campbell & Anderson, 2008).

- *Tertiary intervention:* Within an overall framework of Restorative Classroom Discipline, the model also encompasses individualized interventions and support services likely to be long term and ongoing for that small percentage of the school population (approximately 2 to 5 percent) who present significant and sometimes ongoing behavioral challenges in classrooms and schools. However, for these children as well, intervention is consistent with the principles and practices of restorative practices. One feature that differentiates restorative discipline at this level is that even children who exhibit serious behavioral challenges are not excluded from the school community but are provided support to restore and repair while remaining in school and doing their work. This level of intervention has been referred to as Tier 3 in the special education literature (Walker et al., 1996).

Restorative Classroom Discipline Planning

In schools where there is a commitment to restorative practices, teachers will be involved at various stages of developing the model implemented at your school. There will be many aspects of the framework that are familiar to you, but there will also be areas where you may require further professional development (see Chapter 10). An important first step is to ensure that you contribute to the schoolwide development of restorative practices—not just to the implementation in your classroom. We have provided a Discussion Paper that provides a brief summary of restorative practices that can be used in talking with others about the approach.

Discussion Paper: What is Restorative Classroom Discipline?

Background: Restorative practices in schools have been implemented and internationally guided by Zehr (1990) and others. Restorative classroom practices are based on a restorative justice view that offenses represent conflict between people that is best addressed by working to restore relationships and making things right, not by blaming and punishing with a focus on retribution.

Definition: Restorative discipline reflects a whole-school ethos encompassing principles and practices to support peacemaking and conflict resolution through healing damaged relationships and making amends where harm has been done while preserving the dignity of everyone involved.

Key Features:

- Restorative, not retributive, ethos of inclusion in the school
- Curriculum focus on relationships among staff and students, including support for enhancing skills and understandings for restorative conversations and conflict prevention and resolution
- Restorative policies and practices reflecting a whole-school approach to positive relationships, behavioral challenges, and solving conflict through restorative practices
- Processes for mediation, shuttle mediation, and peer mediation in classrooms and schoolwide
- Processes for restorative meetings, informal conferences, classroom conferences, and formal conferences

- School rules, guidelines, and systems that are transparent and fair in response to incidents and threats that require staff and students to be protected from harm or potential harm
- Supports and resources that ensure student and staff safety and mutual respect

References: McCluskey et al. (2008); Varnham (2008); Zehr (1990).

SUMMARY

This chapter provides an overview of the essential features of schools and classrooms committed to restorative practices. The chapter begins by emphasizing the overall importance of attending to school climate and then introduces Restorative Classroom Discipline as a comprehensive approach to relationships, problem solving, the prevention and peaceful resolution of conflict, and strategies for restoration and making amends where harm has occurred. The next chapter describes the process of setting transparent and fair schoolwide and classroom behavior expectations as well as ensuring that such rules are culturally responsive to today's diverse student population.

2 Behavior Expectations for Schools and Classrooms

This chapter addresses one of the first tasks confronting the teacher: specifying and communicating behavior expectations for your classroom as part of the school community. Nearly every school has a set of rules or guidelines that encompass expectations for students, but some guidelines are more meaningful and interpretable than others. You can test how well the current rules and guidelines at your school are working by answering the following question: *Can the students in the grade levels that I teach state the "rules" for how to behave in the hallway, restroom, etc.?*

Before young people can be expected to show good behavior in the classroom and throughout the school, they need to have a clear understanding of what is expected of them at particular ages. In today's schools, these behavior expectations, or "rules," need to be stated clearly for all school settings including classrooms, halls or walkways, stairs, restrooms, cafeterias, assemblies, libraries, gym/intramural sports facilities, school buses, and any outdoor areas surrounding the school. A school and classrooms with transparent rules that are well understood by all students will have fewer difficulties with "bullying" than one where the principal and school personnel do not assume agency or perhaps even deny all responsibility for what happens in that environment.

Later in the guide, we present a framework for translating "behavior expectations for the school community" into observable behaviors, restorative practices when things have gone wrong, and consequences that are enforced at school whenever students do not meet behavior expectations.

In this chapter, however, it is important to emphasize that *unless you can translate a "behavior expectation" into observable behaviors, they will have little meaning for students and are open to abuse by everyone—including you as the teacher.* Sometimes the rule simply needs to be stated in more behavioral (observable) terms, and sometimes what is required is to break down a word like "appropriate" or "properly" into examples at different ages so that students and adults are clear about what is meant by the rule.

WHAT ARE SCHOOLWIDE BEHAVIOR EXPECTATIONS?

Table 1 presents the behavior expectations at Jarrett Middle School in Hawai'i that were developed through extensive consultation across the school. Before specifying the school's behavioral expectations, Jarrett staff agreed to feature three broad "expectations"—caring, responsible, and always learning. In the table, the behaviors to meet each of these expectations are described for different school environments. Does the table include enough information for children—or even for you as a teacher—to know what is acceptable and what is not? Clarity and consistency are important, particularly as you will be developing with your students a parallel set of expectations for your classrooms. Whatever "rules" you establish within your classroom must be aligned with the rules agreed on across the school as a whole.

Look, for example, at some of the behaviors expected in different areas of the school. The table indicates that in the restroom children demonstrate *caring* by respecting the privacy of others, using toilet and urinals properly, and waiting for one's turn. To demonstrate *responsible*, they are to keep restrooms clean, conserve supplies, and use the restroom for its intended use. Finally, for *always learning*, they should practice good hygiene, wash hands, and throw rubbish in trash cans. How would a seventh grader interpret "keep restrooms clean"? Certain expectations within each box could be elsewhere in the matrix—perhaps "throw rubbish in trash cans" under *always learning* would fit better in the category *responsible* and may even be an example of "keep restrooms clean."

General expectations such as "keeping [a place] clean" require clarification: we don't expect students to actually clean the restroom, but we do expect them to clean up after themselves and not leave a mess for the next person. While this may appear to be commonsense, it is appropriate in some cultures to squat on the toilet seat, which leaves footprints and a dirty toilet seat for the next person who may be more likely to sit on the seat. Who communicates with children about these expectations, and how does this occur? Our schools have increasingly multiethnic student populations,

Table 1 Behavior Expectations at Jarrett Middle School

	All Settings	Stairwell/ Walkways	Restrooms	Cafeteria	Assembly	Library	Intramural/ Gym
CARING	• Be on time and on task. • Respect the rights and opinions of others. • Work cooperatively. • Use a quiet voice. • Be courteous and patient. • Report any unsafe conditions or students.	• Respect school property. • Be polite and considerate of others.	• Respect privacy of others. • Use toilet and urinals properly. • Wait your turn.	• Be courteous and patient. • Speak quietly. • Keep your place in line.	• Applaud and cheer appropriately. • Be courteous and patient.	• Use a quiet voice. • Be respectful and patient. • Wait in line to be helped.	• Applaud/ cheer appropriately. • Be courteous and patient.
RESPONSIBLE	• Bring required supplies. • Complete assignments on time. • Be prepared for class. • Follow classroom rules. • Make good choices. • Take care of outstanding obligations.	• Practice safe behavior. (Walk.) • Avoid loitering in stairwell. • Remain on ground floor during noninstructional times. • Keep school environment clean.	• Keep restrooms clean. • Conserve supplies. • Use restroom for its intended use.	• Walk at all times. • Use your own picture ID. • Keep area clean. • Empty trays and milk properly.	• Pay attention to speaker/ performer. • Enter/leave in an orderly manner. • Sit in assigned seat. • Keep area clean.	• Return books on time. • Follow library rules and procedures. • Know your AR reading level and user number. • Take care of library materials.	• Follow gym rules. • Enter/leave in an orderly manner. • Take care of and return equipment. • Attend scheduled games.
ALWAYS	• Practice appropriate behavior. • Keep on task. • Participate in classroom activities. • Follow directions and all safety rules.	• Practice appropriate behavior. • Use appropriate language.	• Practice good hygiene. • Wash hands. • Throw rubbish in trash cans.	• Practice proper table manners.	• Practice active listening and proper social etiquette.	• Ask for assistance. • Learn to use available/ new resources.	• Participate in activity. • Follow instructions and all safety rules.

yet their basic structures and systems may be very monocultural—putting some students at ease and challenging others whose culture differs markedly from the dominant mainstream culture. It is easy to forget the extent to which we rely on ongoing socialization to teach children things like "restroom rules," which may not, in fact, be universally understood.

Wherever there is a risk for bullying, having clear expectations expressed through observable behaviors is particularly important. In Chapter 5, bullying is discussed in detail but an examination of the Jarrett School's list of expectations for all settings is in order: Do they rule out bullying behavior, or would another set of rules be needed to cover instances of bullying? Ideally, these behavior expectations should preclude bullying and not require another layer of "rules" to prevent behavior problems and abuse. In the insert, we provide two examples of how very general expectations can be rephrased in specific ways to prevent and intervene with bullying.

Examples for Bullying Prevention and Intervention: Instructions about how to demonstrate *Caring* in the classroom specific to preventing bullying.

	Stairwell/Walkways—general and nonspecific	Classroom—more specific and oriented towards antibullying
Caring:	• Respect school property. • Be polite and considerate of others.	• Respect textbooks and other materials and report damage. • Invite a classmate who doesn't have close friends in class to walk with you to the next class. • Ask for help from a teacher if you see someone being bullied.

Your Role in Developing the School's Behavior Expectations

Your school develops a set of schoolwide behavior expectations and involves teachers at various stages in the process. First, the school principal invites the school community to identify high level principles for schoolwide "expectations" such as the ones identified for the Jarrett School (caring, responsible, always learning). The issue is raised for discussion on the agenda of one or more school staff meetings and an announcement made at school assembly inviting students to make suggestions. Most likely, a suggestion box is available outside the school office for ideas about "Behavior Expectations for [My School]." A senior teacher serves as "Project Manager" in charge of this process, and the planning committee should consist of at least one interested teacher, a behavioral support specialist or district resource person, and a parent from the school community.

It is crucial for teachers to engage in this process, given their knowledge about reasonable expectations for children at different ages. This committee takes a blank chart with the broad framework included in the example for Jarrett Middle School and works on filling in the cells with possible statements about expectations. Following discussions across the school, the committee prepares a revised, final version for wide distribution across the school community. As a teacher, you'll are invited to comment and to discuss the draft with your students to get their ideas. The school then develops a flyer that students can take home with them to share with their families, and as appropriate throughout the school, there are posted displays of the Behavior Expectations.

Over time, teachers as well as all other school personnel review the set of Behavior Expectations and sample observable behaviors to ensure that they reflect ongoing needs, issues, and concerns. Your school might review these annually, inviting recommendations for changes based on systematic analysis of behavioral issues and incidents throughout the year.

Developing Behavior Expectations for Your Classroom

In addition to schoolwide behavior expectations, teachers have a more specific set of behavior expectations for their own classrooms. At the elementary school level, this set of rules is established with the students at the very start of the school year and posted in a prominent place in the classroom. In middle and high schools, where students change classes every period, a teacher establishes a set of rules that covers all classes taught by that teacher. Typically, a teacher identifies no more than five or six of these rules, ranging from general to specific. A typical example for an elementary school classroom might be the following:

- Respect my teacher, classmates, and guests entering the room
- Do my work
- Keep my hands to myself
- Help one another
- Respect property

The following variation was observed on the board in a science classroom in a large urban high school:

- Be prepared for class
- Respect yourself and others (this includes ideas and property)
- Follow all directions given by the teacher
- Follow all the rules of Anywhere High School
- Have fun and learn as much as possible every day

In many classrooms where cooperative learning is used frequently, a common rule is "no put-downs." For most of the posted classroom rules we have seen, there are some aspects that appear regularly, such as coming to class prepared, respecting self and others, following directions, taking care of property, and referring to learning. Teachers can and often do put their personal flavor on these rules such as the last one above in the science class that tells students to "have fun and learn as much as possible every day."

We advocate that teachers involve the students themselves in the process of setting up these classroom rules. Most teachers do this, so our advice is not particularly earth-shattering. An important reason to discuss class rules with the students and involve them in the process is that this calls attention to the schoolwide rules that exist for everyone while also pointing out that there can and will be special rules for particular places in the school in addition to these rules—such as in the science lab, or the English classroom in high school, or in a particular third-grade teacher's classroom. This enables children to become increasingly aware of how different environments, settings, and circumstances within those places demand different behavioral responses: for example, we observed a classroom where the teacher established four levels of noise that were readily understood and, upon saying the number, the students knew what was meant—Level 1 was outside voices, Level 2 was hallway voices, Level 3 was in-class discussion voices, and Level 4 was quiet voices during work. This teacher could tell the students that they needed to use Level 4 when working in their groups, Level 3 when the groups came together for class discussion, and could say quite simply "be careful that you're not using Level 2 voices!" when things got too loud.

A second, equally important reason to discuss the classroom rules with students is to develop a sense of communal ownership for those rules. Each teacher is likely to have a set of basic rules that he or she does not want to compromise but could additionally encourage the students in each class to develop one or two additional rules themselves. Involving students in the process of developing the rules and taking major responsibility for some rules of their own enhances their sense of responsibility in enforcing and adhering to the rules. The process of discussion helps students to better understand the nature of such rules and why they are important. The discussion also helps the teacher to understand his or her students and their ideas about classroom community. Finally, students may suggest rules that the teacher might have missed but which are important to them and which would make them feel safe and welcome.

In Syracuse, New York, an elementary school experimented with implementation of a rule modeled after Vivian Paley's book, *You Can't Say*

You Can't Play, which was called the YCSYCP rule (Paley, 1992). Vivian Paley is a children's author who was for many years a kindergarten teacher at the University of Chicago's laboratory school; her book reporting the results of this "rule" at that school was the inspiration for an applied research project carried out by a university professor and four elementary school teachers (Sapon-Shevin, Dobbelaere, Corrigan, Goodman, & Mastin, 1998). There are various formal programs designed to build character, create community, improve the classroom climate, prevent conflict, and teach children how to be good citizens, take responsibility, and acquire the skills for democracy. A far less formal rule such as "you can't say you can't play" supplements those efforts but, in a very real sense, could also be closer to home in translating higher level principles down to the level of children's daily play and social interactions.

In her book, Paley describes her concerns about how children in her kindergarten class and other classes were excluded with statements like "You can't play with us" and "You're not my best friend anymore." As a teacher, she decided to raise the issue with her class in a discussion about friendships, connections, and exclusion by asking them what they thought about having the rule "You can't say you can't play." She asked her students two key questions: (1) Is the rule fair? and (2) Would the rule work? Paley then went throughout the school and met with other classes to talk about such a rule, asking the same two questions. Paley discusses what the children thought about the rule at different levels rather than experimenting with implementation of the rule and describing what happened. As a university researcher, Sapon-Shevin met with four elementary teachers who indicated they were interested in participatory research to investigate implementation of the rule in their kindergarten, first-, second-, and fourth-grade classrooms. Their book chapter describes this process and the results with the children.

The school where this work was carried out—Ed Smith Elementary School—covered Grades K–7 and enrolled approximately 800 students in 35 classrooms at the time of the study. The school was well known for its inclusion of students with significant disabilities, particularly those with autism, and the student population at this urban school included a range of socioeconomic, religious, and ethnic backgrounds. The four teachers explained why they wanted to participate in a project that would support children's social relationships:

Anne (kindergarten): *I like children helping children as opposed to adults helping children. They are so capable if they are given the chance. Helping others teaches them to be sensitive to others' needs now and in their later years. I think kindergarten lays the foundation for social and academic success for all children. (p. 109)*

Mary (first grade): *I've always been interested in watching and supporting the social interactions of children. These are skills they are going to need throughout their lives and the foundations are formed at an early age. Sometimes patterns of exclusion get started in younger grades and then continue on in the older grades. This is a rule that I've always used in my head when supporting students but never explicitly stated. I thought it was a rule kids could understand and accept. (p. 111)*

Kathy (second grade): *When I heard about the project, I immediately thought what a great opportunity to have more "ammunition" to fight put-downs and exclusion as it typically goes on in the classroom . . . . Two stories from my own childhood that had a profound impact on me were "The Ugly Ducking" and "Rudolph the Red-Nosed Reindeer." When I heard the words "you can't say you can't play," a light bulb went on in my head and my heart!" (p. 112)*

Cathleen (fourth grade): *I can't imagine having to go to a place either as an adult or a kid where I didn't feel that I'd be accepted or I'd be safe, where I couldn't say what I thought and nobody was going to put me down, where I could acknowledge that I don't understand the directions or that I don't know how to do this or that it would not be okay to ask for some help or that I could give help to somebody else and it would be okay. I just couldn't imagine that. . . . I [wondered] if older children would be considered able to respond to this new "rule." It seemed to be the perfect fit for our classroom. It was simply an extension of what we were trying to do. (p. 113)*

Each of the teachers had different approaches to how they implemented and used the rule across the two school years for which results were recorded. In her second-grade classroom, for example, Kathy gave the children many journal writing assignments linked to the rule, such as asking them to "Tell me about a time when someone told *you* that you couldn't play. How did you feel?" or "Tell me about a time when you told someone they couldn't play. How did you feel? How did the other person feel?" The questions were also discussed in small groups and whole-class meetings. Anne described how she introduced the rule to her kindergarten students at a class meeting but ensured there would be modeling so that the children would know how to actually ask to join a group. For example, at lunchtime she would ask a table of children in the cafeteria if she could join them, and other adults would do the same. She had her students enact common scenarios that focused on problems with sharing. These approaches worked well precisely because role-play and problem solving were already models used in Anne's classroom for various activities.

The fourth-grade teacher also confronted the challenges associated with her students' interactions with other fourth graders whose classes did not share the rule and what to do in fifth grade when they would be separated into five different classes with many students who had no previous history with the rule. At this grade level, the rule raised various other issues for the students: is it right to "force" children to play with other children even if they aren't friends? Are there situations and structures that limit the number of persons who can participate, and how does the rule apply to those instances (e.g., limited number of players in a game or at a learning station)? And how does the rule apply to the wider society where most people have no experience with the rule and may not agree with it? These are complex social issues, and the teacher felt that these discussions benefited students and helped them to think at a very practical level about the meanings of citizenship and social relationships. Mary explained:

> *The rule set a tone in the classroom. It was plainly stated and understood. This helps us quickly cut through some of the artificial reasons why social situations break down with first graders. This then leads logically to the next step—we are all going to play or work here so what do we need to do to help everyone be part of this situation? The real work of social problem solving and interaction can begin.* (p. 125)

Sapon-Shevin and her teacher colleagues conclude that the rule serves as a powerful organizing principle for the classroom, bringing to life the principle of inclusion in the reality of social interaction practice. The rule was also not a cure-all, and the teachers described the many ways in which they explored its meanings and applications with the children themselves. Rather than seeing this as a disadvantage or a limitation, the authors maintain that awareness of inconsistencies of certain values across different environments helps children to see the implications and challenges associated with democratic principles and practices designed to be fair. Precisely because the "rule" wasn't universally adopted (even within this one school) the children were required to explore different solutions when confronted with unfairness and exclusion.

SUMMARY

This chapter provides an overview of developing and supporting school-wide behavior expectations that are realistic for children across the ages represented in the school population. The processes described here are designed to ensure full school involvement in the development of a transparent set of behavior expectations. A model is also presented that teachers can use to develop rules for their classrooms in a way designed to ensure that children regard those rules as transparent, fair, and reasonable. The next chapter, for use in school by teachers, addresses home-school relationships, including strategies to establish ongoing positive interactions with families that enhance and contribute to students' learning and behavior.

3 Home-School and Community Relationships

This chapter addresses the nature of the relationship between home and school and between the teacher and the school community, especially as it relates to the parents of the students in your classroom. The relationships that teachers establish with students' families and the community are at the core of restorative practices, which work best where there is mutual trust, respect, and understanding before problems and challenges emerge. The concept of intercultural competence is introduced, and strategies are described for teachers to enhance their capacities to interact positively with students and families from different cultural and linguistic groups. Suggestions are provided for establishing ongoing home-school partnership relationships to better support learning and behavior for all students as well as to provide the context for working constructively with students who have particular behavioral challenges.

ESTABLISHING POSITIVE HOME-SCHOOL RELATIONSHIPS

The relationship between home, school, and community sets the tone for restorative practices. For the teacher, relationship building is the first step to restorative practices, and how the school communicates its schoolwide commitment to this ethos is discussed in Chapter 1. Generally, when communications are going well with families and parents then addressing individual issues is easier and there is less scope for misunderstandings and mistrust. If a parent's first real interaction with the teacher is because an incident has occurred, parents can experience that contact as adversarial even with the best of intentions on the teacher's part. Parents may feel that they are being blamed or are expected to solve ongoing major issues that they are already struggling with. They may feel alienated or intimidated by the teacher's professional status and dominant cultural identity; this is a particular risk whenever the family speaks a first language other than English and/or the teacher and the family come from different cultural backgrounds. Also remember that parents are influenced by their own childhood experiences with school. If that memory of school is negative, then from the moment of that first contact by the teacher or school principal, the parent can be susceptible to mistrust and adopt a defensive posture.

For all these reasons, a behavioral incident should never be the occasion for the first contact. Teachers must work to establish positive communications with every child's parents from the very beginning of school, before significant behavior problems emerge, requiring a first teacher-parent interaction focused on conflict. Whenever a positive relationship has not yet been established with a student's family—for whatever reason—how the teacher approaches family members can still have a huge impact on their ability to respond positively and constructively.

Approaches to Home-School Interactions

The family and the school can see a situation quite differently and most likely have different perspectives and priorities that interfere with efforts to address problems, especially if driven underground rather than acknowledged. Glynn, Berryman, Bidois, and Atvars (1997) describe a strategy for parents, teachers, and the students themselves to identify and evaluate their own priorities and what they see as major issues. The teacher, parents, and students start the process by completing parallel checklists that ask them to respond to three questions:

1. What are "problem contexts" for students at home and at school?

2. What specific behaviors "bother us" at home and at school?

3. What are the "behaviors we like to see" at home or school?

The lists were done independently, and the three lists were collated to identify areas of agreement and disagreement that could be discussed by everyone.

Interestingly, the process identified factors that do have serious intervention implications. Students were the only ones to identify the school bus and being out with friends as problem contexts; school staff were the only ones to identify the lunchroom and school field trips as problem contexts; and parents were the only ones to mention getting up as a problem context. Everyone named homework as a problem context. For problem behaviors, there was agreement that teasing/taunting, shouting/yelling, not listening or following instructions were problems, but teachers alone mentioned bullying and only parents mentioned tantrums. For most valued behaviors, all three groups named caring, sharing, good personal care, and being responsible. Family members and students agreed that choosing friends carefully was valued, and students and teachers agreed that listening, supporting, and playing together were valued. Only students mentioned being on time; only teachers mentioned getting involved; and only family members mentioned showing respect for one's own and other people's property.

This process allows the main participants—students, teachers, and family members—to identify the behaviors and contexts that are important and challenging to them. Having this information before discipline events occur in a classroom is helpful and can provide an important framework for discussing an incident. Accordingly, participants who are at a meeting to consider constructively what to do about a problem have prior useful knowledge about areas of shared values as well as areas of disagreement. This is in contrast to traditional processes that are more likely to foreground only one perspective—usually that of school personnel—to drive intervention planning. If only one perspective is legitimized, the other participants are disempowered and likely to resist agency or responsibility for the intervention.

Teachers can use this process to identify for themselves and also find out from their students and families what they see as valued behavior, problematic behavior, and situations that put them at risk. With the objective of better understandings of different perspectives, teachers can discuss with both parents and students particular areas of agreement and disagreement not with the purpose of forcing new lists that reflect artificial agreement, but rather to acknowledge differences to be worked through as part of the process. Such a process can be the starting point for an anti bullying initiative or a framework for positive teacher-parent conferencing. The strategy is particularly effective as a starting point for individual conferencing with family members on behalf of students whose behavior signals the need for more intensive interventions.

CULTURE, CONTEXT, AND INTERCULTURAL COMPETENCE

Culturally and linguistically diverse (CLD) students can be at risk in so-called mainstream schools that are not really so much mainstream as they are reflective of one dominant culture, such as the culture of those who are of Western European descent in the United States. Despite massive changes in the demographic characteristics of students, the structure of schools hasn't changed a great deal for many decades. In ever increasing numbers, students who speak English as an alternative (not their first) language, and students who are immigrants or even refugees from international conflict regions now populate schools in countries such as the United States, Britain, Australia, Canada, and New Zealand. In many urban schools in the United States and Britain, the majority of the student population is not descended from Western Europe but instead encompass diverse cultural groups, including African, Hispanic, Asian, Pacific Nation, and Eastern European. Countries such as the United States and Australia also have indigenous peoples whose presence predates white colonists, who eventually established schools characterized by teaching and learning that is very western-oriented. These more individualistic and competitive models of schooling are quite unlike the collectivist values and practices of indigenous peoples in particular, resulting in cultural mismatches between school achievement expectations and community perspectives.

Cultural Mismatches Between Home and School

Harry (2008) discussed the issue of cultural and linguistic mismatches between the families of children receiving special education services and educational personnel. She critiques special education requirements and systems that reflect dominant culture values, including using formality, requiring extensive legal and written documents, and catering to well-educated parents who speak English as their first language. It is an established fact that CLD learners are disproportionately referred for special education services, labeled as having disabilities such as emotional disturbance and behavioral disorders, and suspended and excluded from school for behavior (Cartledge & Kourea, 2008; Skiba et al., 2008; Vincent & Tobin, 2011). These disproportions reflect cultural mainstreams, which advantage children who match that mainstream—those who are white and middle class—and disadvantage children whose culturally and linguistic identities are different and hence "minoritized" by the identity of the school (Shields, Bishop, & Mazawi, 2005). Cultural differences can have particular consequences for judgments about behavior. What is inappropriate for one cultural identity may be more acceptable in another. Whenever schools are setting general behavioral expectations, it is important to seek advice from community constituents who are knowledgeable about the mores of different cultural groups represented in the school. There may be some teachers whose cultural and linguistic identity matches that of some of the students, but teachers also may have become so acculturated to the school's dominant mainstream culture that they are no longer in tune with important cultural differences.

A particular risk for minoritized cultures is that schools and professionals come to view children and their families from CLD groups as having *deficits* rather than recognizing cultural differences (Bishop, 2011). A child may be seen entirely from a *deficit theorizing perspective* when in fact that student is simply displaying behaviors that are encouraged and valued outside school. Deficit perspectives can also mean that dominant culture professionals ignore or are unaware of the students' strengths. There may also be communication obstacles for a teacher whose multiple identities differ from those of students and their families; teachers are professional educators, whereas the family plays the role of child advocate. The teacher's values, socioeconomic status, sexual orientation, and cultural and linguistic background may differ from that of students and their families. Consequently, there may be subtle barriers that seem irrelevant to educational issues but that actually profoundly disadvantage some children and some families unless they are acknowledged and addressed. Responsibility for addressing potential cultural mismatches has to fall on the teacher who is the professional in the picture and has access to multiple supports and professional services to build constructive relationships with diverse school communities.

Culturally Competent Teachers

Teachers and other professionals in schools must be culturally competent, defined broadly as the ability to interact with persons from different cultural groups (Sue, 1998). Teachers' first steps in building positive home-school relationships is learning about students' home communities and developing their own expertise and experience with diverse cultures. Professionals working together in schools have multiple opportunities to build relationships with one another, which translate into a comfortable background to their work over time. We take these relationships for granted rather than acknowledging how important they are to our ability to engage as a team in the daily work of educators. It is easy to forget that while school professionals bring their ongoing relationships to meetings, families and children typically come to such meetings "cold" are yet expected to engage openly in discussions about issues that are highly emotional, stressful, embarrassing, and perhaps even shameful for them. In indigenous and many other cultures, it is not acceptable to get "down to business" unless the time is taken first to learn about one another and develop a basic level of comfort within an interaction. Thus, start case conferencing meetings that simply introduce people by name and then launch immediately into discussions of problems represent a fundamental power differential that advantages the professionals and puts the family on the 'back foot.' For example, educators consider that Individualized Education Program (IEP) meetings are a positive model for parent involvement in planning educational interventions. For families, these kinds of formal meetings without any background relationships among participants can instead be disempowering (Harry, 2008).

Savage (2009) noted that behavioral specialists in New Zealand working with indigenous Māori students and their families are expected to take the time to get to know the family on neutral turf and to show interest in the family's perspective on the issues. Glynn et al. (1997) describe one process for initiating a student, teacher, and family partnership in behavioral interventions. The process begins not with a formal meeting to discuss the problem. Instead, the family is invited to visit the school and observe a particular cultural event of interest to them. Of course, a process such as this won't work if the school is not supporting any such events reflecting the different cultural constituents within the school population!

There is a growing literature on culturally responsive schooling and pedagogy to guide educators in the process of becoming culturally competent (Gay, 2010; Sleeter & Grant, 2009; Sleeter, 2011). Every teacher needs to self-assess his or her own intercultural competence and take advantage of professional development opportunities to acquire new skills and understandings so that the inevitable cultural mismatches do not unfairly disadvantage and discriminate against children and their families. Chapter 4 describes in more detail how teachers can demonstrate cultural competence and culturally responsive pedagogies in the classroom, focusing on empirical research that has identified specific teacher behaviors and characteristics that can be developed as part of professional practice. The professional development self-assessment tool in Chapter 10 provides further guidance for the process of building the necessary skills and understandings.

HOME-SCHOOL PARTNERSHIPS

There is extensive research literature on building home-school partnerships as a way of improving students' learning and academic performance (Bull, Brooking, & Campbell, 2008). This research suggests that successful partnerships are focused on learning and other clear academic goals. However, this should not represent a unilateral perspective in supporting the work of the school rather than being equally for the benefit of the family. For example, suggesting that parents monitor or help with homework may sound like a good idea, one that for teachers seems a natural way to support children's learning within the context of a parent-child learning interaction. Confronting parents with an expectation that they help their child with homework can instead increase parent-child conflict and make parents feel inadequate. It is very important that issues and difficulties faced by some families be recognized: what looks like family noninvolvement with school should not be interpreted as evidence that the parents do not value education or care about their children's learning. Home-school partnerships must be genuine partnerships and not seen simply as an opportunity to assist the school with its own goals and tasks.

Home-School Relationships and Behavioral Challenges

A respectful and equitable collaboration between home and school is especially important when the concern is about behavior. This is partly because home and family circumstances could well be contributing to emotional disorders that are manifest at school. It is also because, regardless of the causes, challenging behavior will only be addressed if those important in the child's life—such as parents—are on board with the plans. It is difficult to engage families if they are distrustful of the school, hostile towards teachers, and unwilling to reflect on the possible contribution they may be making to students' difficulties. This is why establishing effective and constructive communication with parents prior to escalation of behavioral challenges is so very important.

Teachers should not feel that they need to be equal partners with parents in the sense that they are the same—the roles are very different and the teacher is the educational and developmental expert. The available research emphasizes that this partnership must start off with effective communication and mutual regard (Molloy, Fleming, Rodriguez, Saavedra, Tucker, & Williams, 1995). As Minke and Anderson (2005) note, many teachers will not have formal training in working with families; thus a practical guide such as one by Christenson and Sheridan (2001) is strongly recommended. A few pointers that are especially relevant to the principles behind restorative processes include:

- When families, especially two parents, are interacting with you together, it is not uncommon in some cultures for the man to let the woman speak and to say little himself. In other cultures, it may be the man who speaks and the woman who remains silent. Take a moment to evaluate whether there might be a broader cultural reason behind differential speaking behavior at a meeting. Even if the reason isn't a cultural one but is based on personal differences, there is no need to put the more reticent family members on the spot by asking them to articulate their opinion in addition to what a family spokesperson has just said.

- Of course, parents may not agree on the nature of a problem and its solution. Expect that there will be some degree of tension among family members, who may blame each other and make accusations. It is not your responsibility to resolve these differences, and it is often best to steer conversations away from topics of blame or culpability. Instead, simply keep focusing on possible solutions to a problem by creating new motivations for positive rather than negative behavior.

- Often you will be interacting with blended families, which may involve stepparents and foster parents or both. Be cautious of making assumptions about family structures and dynamics different from your own. Many, if not most children, no longer live in the stereotypical stable, middle-class family home once considered essential to support children properly. Various family arrangements can and do represent positive opportunities for interpersonal growth.

- Most intervention plans rely on mediators to make them work. Try to ascertain who it is in the family who really has the most influence over the student under discussion. The student might look up to a grandparent, an older brother, an aunt, or even a close family friend.

- Listen carefully; resist the urge to adopt the teacher role and be in charge. Be careful of your language so that it never sounds like you are accusing the parents of something, even when it seems obvious that they are contributing directly to the problem.

- For many families there are practical barriers to implementing even simple plans—lack of time, lack of resources, stress, and so on. Make sure that suggested changes are in keeping with what families are really capable of achieving.

- Prior to a formal meeting try to explain very briefly (over the phone or by text message) what it is you hope to achieve—that the focus is on allowing the student of concern to be the best that he can be. Parents are often summoned to school meetings to be criticized or to be given bad news about their child. Based on their past experiences, they may approach the proposed partnership with hesitation or anger. Diffuse this by your willingness to listen and even acknowledge mistakes (such as admitting that you came on too strong with the child, thus contributing further to his feeling of being treated unjustly).

- At the end of a discussion, ask one member of the family (typically the person who has been spokesperson) to summarize mutually agreed-on conclusions. Together, list the actual tasks agreed to at the meeting.

Strategies to Build Home-School Partnerships

Some years ago, Evans and colleagues conducted a project to improve home-school communications in a large upstate New York school district (Evans, Okifuji, & Thomas, 1995). They saw a disconcerting tendency by both teachers and parents to blame one another for the child who was behaving badly and becoming a problem in the classroom—the teachers blamed the family, and the family blamed the school! While it is not possible for both arguments to be correct, there was usually a little truth on both sides. Some parents do not consider that education has any value for them, particularly if they did not like school themselves, were made to feel unwelcome in school, are described as being poor disciplinarians, or have problems of their own, such as a serious emotional disorder (like depression). There are some parents who are overtly abusive, punitive, and neglectful of their children. On the other hand, parents sometimes told us that they never had a positive interaction with their child's teacher, never received a friendly little note, were called on the phone only when there was a problem, and heard reports from their child about the many times that he or she had been dealt with harshly or unfairly by school authorities.

Given these histories and beliefs, it might seem obvious that the conflict or tension between home and school can be fairly simply resolved by a few inexpensive and easily and quickly deployed strategies. We are going to provide a menu of things that the *teacher* can do, but we do not mean to imply that families should not share in the responsibility. It is just that families are often under considerable emotional and financial distress, whereas it is the teacher who is the professional and who is in a position to facilitate change. So we list these as one-sided suggestions that are not dependent on the parents or caregivers making the first move or even reciprocating right away with gratitude or increased cooperation. In our experience, these positive changes do eventually occur—basically one has to recognize that all parents ultimately want what is best for their children. However, there is no point waiting for the parents to make the first move or to show a sudden new level of cooperation. At the end of the day, the goal is improved communication and interaction with parents and families, which is critical if serious and complex behavior problems are ever to be resolved. We need parents to be part of the solution, not part of the problem. This is especially crucial when relying on the collaborative processes, acceptance, forgiveness, and renewed sense of fairness that is inherent in the restorative model.

So what can be done to improve home-school communication and to develop collaborative relationships in which everyone is working together for the sake of the student? Listed below are some simple strategies suitable for elementary school. Chances are that you are already doing some or all of these useful things:

- Find some excuse to send a positive note home, or phone the parents, or send them a text that simply focuses on some small accomplishment by the student. For each of your students, keep a personal record where you record every positive and every negative communication with their home. Make certain that there is a balance of positive versus negative interactions for each and every child in your room.

- Arrange a meeting with parents, not to discuss a problem but simply to get to know them. Recognize that they might really dislike coming to the school or cannot come during convenient school hours or might not have or be able to afford transportation. Instead, suggest a meeting at the local diner or McDonald's.

- Work with your school to develop a "backpack program." The one we used was simply an inexpensive brightly colored backpack that each student took turns taking home. The backpack had some permanent items and some that the students were allowed to take out and leave at home. Teachers are often surprised at how many low-income families simply do not have things like colored markers, coloring books, and story books at home. The backpacks can later contain items for parents such as parenting tips, how to use praise, fun activities to do with your child, and so on.

- Have a class newsletter—make certain every child gets mentioned, not just the stars.

- Get to know families by setting aside class time for students to talk about positive events happening in their family: Mom is having a baby; Dad's away with the National Guard; a stepdad bought a new tool. If students raise serious family issues, don't discuss them in class but be sure to set aside some time to allow them to talk to you privately (see Chapter 4 for further details).

- Make certain your school is seen as a community resource—just how comfortable is it for parents from many different social and ethnic backgrounds to simply drop in and not feel demeaned in any way?

You will note that there is a certain commonality to these ideas: respect parents no matter how difficult they may seem, find ways of connecting that do not emphasize the potential power differential, and celebrate each family's strengths publicly in the classroom.

At the intermediate and high school levels, things are slightly different because parents are gradually having less influence as the adolescent negotiates increasing levels of autonomy. But although they try to act independent, most adolescents—even those about to graduate from school—are still surprisingly dependent emotionally on parental approval and support. Some of the following strategies are possible:

- Give the student tangible recognition for improved work. Even seemingly hardened teenagers can appreciate getting stickers (even smiley faces!) on their work that they may take home and show their parents (Bishop, 2011; Sleeter, 2011).
- Develop a collaborative project where parents can contribute their skills or their labor. In our rural upstate New York community, the parents helped teens build a barn to be used by the local 4-H club. On another occasion, the school conducted a beautification program with some talented parents contributing by painting a mural.
- If you are teaching English or History or Social Studies, ask students to get together with a parent or caregiver to coauthor a short history of their family—or anything interesting about their background. Let them know that these will be circulated (in order not to embarrass anyone, you might want to edit them a bit!) in the class newsletter or class Facebook page if you have one. Get to know their cultures, religions, and occupations.
- Early in the school year, design a totally different sort of parent night. Most such occasions are a bit stiff, and parents dread them. Ask your students to design an event that parents would find entertaining—have an auction (you might need to get a local business to donate a prize), have a pizza night, show an unusual but educational DVD, sponsor a careers night where parent volunteers provide the career models rather than bringing in outsiders.
- Be sure you know the make up of who is living at home. Blended or solo-parent families are as common as nuclear biological families living in a home with a picket fence. Have all relevant mobile phone numbers and send group texts. Know how to pronounce the names of parents correctly and whether the mother and father might have different surnames. At the beginning of the year send every family a brief introduction about yourself that includes something personal like your favorite hobbies, and include your goals for the school

year. Tell them about the school's commitment to restorative discipline throughout the school and in your classroom.

The key point is that you must never wait for a crisis, an emergency, or a significant emotional problem to occur before making initial contact with a student's family. When behavior problems escalate, you can be reasonably confident that things are not going well at home; you need to have some inkling of family dynamics, who is respected in the extended family, how you can get hold of parents quickly without making it seem like a crisis. Never report a problem that has occurred at school without knowing as much of the details and the different perspectives as you can possibly gather; avoid reporting a problem unless you have a reasonable idea of how the parent will react—either towards you or the student. Don't assume that the family will be on your side—they may have a long history of negative interactions with the school and personal histories of school failure themselves that make it almost impossible for them to approach the building without feeling sadness, shame, or anger.

SUMMARY

This chapter addresses interactions among home, school, and community with a focus on how the teacher can develop positive relationships with each student's family. Key approaches to home-school relationships are highlighted consistent with restorative practices, which work best in contexts supporting mutual trust, respect, and understanding between home and school prior to the emergence of problems and serious incidents. Principles and practices for intercultural competence are introduced, requiring acknowledgment that schools typically represent a dominant culture despite the presence of multiple cultural identities among teachers, students, and the community. The chapter also includes suggestions for establishing positive, ongoing home-school partnerships that support all students and are restorative in nature. Next, we focus on how to ensure that the classroom provides the framework for promoting positive learning and behavior. Beginning with Chapter 4, we address issues such as classroom climate, culturally responsive pedagogies, and strategies to support student learning and behavior in the regular classroom.

Section II

Putting the Model in Place

4 Classroom Climate and Cultural Responsiveness

T he first section of this chapter covers the climate of the classroom and ways in which the teacher communicates high expectations to students within a caring community. Examples are provided for establishing a warm classroom climate at the elementary and secondary levels. The chapter also addresses teaching styles and culturally responsive practices to ensure positive relationships with students from diverse cultural and linguistic backgrounds that may differ from the dominant school culture. The content of the chapter provides an overview of the variety of regular education practices that benefit all students and create the foundation for positive learning and behavior.

ESTABLISHING A WARM CLASSROOM CLIMATE

This guide is not focused solely on ordinary, everyday classroom control—although having good, working behavior management and restorative practices creates the foundation needed for all students; it is primarily concerned with managing the behavior of that usually small group of students whose actions far exceed the expected level of occasional misbehavior and disobedience that might be seen in many children. However, it is difficult for a teacher to implement an effective intervention plan for the more exceptionally difficult behaviors if there is not a structure in which students typically follow classroom rules, settle quickly, get on with assigned tasks, work collaboratively in groups, and transition in a responsible manner from one setting or activity to another. In other words, the general atmosphere or *climate* of the classroom must be positive: the teacher does not need to raise his or her voice too often, directives are focused on learning and not on conduct, and reprimands are rare. A positive classroom climate is one where students are engaged, enjoy being in the class, like and respect the teacher, understand and acknowledge the essential rules for the classroom (and may well have contributed to their specifications), respect values such as fairness and empathy, and appreciate the rights of all students in the class to equitable treatment. In classrooms with a positive climate, all students feel they belong and are accepted.

A positive classroom climate establishes the context needed for effective interventions with individual students. In addition, positive relationships between the teacher and students (and hence a positive class climate) have significant implications for managing emotions and increasing a student's *emotion competence*. Emotion competence is a construct similar to what is known more popularly as emotional intelligence (EQ) (Goleman, 1995). EQ is thought to be made up of several component skills, the most important of which are:

- *Self and other awareness*: understanding and identifying feelings; recognizing that one's actions have consequences in terms of others' feelings
- *Mood management*: handling and managing difficult feelings; controlling impulses; and handling anger constructively
- *Being self-motivated*: the ability to set goals and persevere with optimism and hope, even when faced with setbacks
- *Empathy*: being able to put yourself "in someone else's shoes"; being able to take another individual's perspective and show genuine caring
- *Contributing to relationships*: making friends; resolving conflicts; cooperating; collaborative learning

Emotionally competent students show prosocial behavior and social skills, which in turn leads to fewer instances of bullying, aggression, and disruptive behavior. There are many different types of challenging behaviors with different functions and complex origins and causes. However, at the heart of many behavior disorders is an emotional need. The most common needs are (a) difficulty with managing feelings of anger and frustration; (b) poor coping skills when faced with emotionally difficult situations; (c) poor impulse control and a focus on immediate gratification; (d) excessive need for attention or recognition or feelings of importance; (e) strong desire to please peers and so unable to resist peer pressure; (f) feeling anxious (security is easily threatened) or hopeless, feeling worthless or unable to perform as well as others; (g) having difficulty judging social-emotional situations and making incorrect inferences about other students' intentions; and (h) having callous disregard for the feelings of others and thus disposed to exploit peers sexually or through physical aggression. By listing these in negative terms as we have just done, there is a risk of undermining one really important point: all of these characteristics relate to a lack of emotional skills that are more likely to be acquired at school than anywhere else. A classroom that is sensitive to emotion learning provides a myriad of natural opportunities to develop emotional competence.

Positive class climate is related to improved student academic outcomes, reduction in internalizing behavior disorders, enhanced student social and emotion competence, greater engagement and motivation to learn, reduced teacher victimization, and improved attendance (Gottfredson, Gottfredson, & Payne, 2005). Negative classroom climate has been shown to relate to aggression and social-emotional difficulties (Gazelle, 2006; Somersalo, Solantaus, & Almqvist, 2002). In Table 2 we reproduce an example from the Center for Comprehensive School Reform and Improvement (2009) that shows how an important emotional climate variable—establishing a strong sense of belonging—was part of a more general, schoolwide disciplinary plan addressing disproportionate suspension statistics by ethnicity.

Table 2 Disproportionality in Suspensions

The challenge

The suspension and discipline records showed that there was an overrepresentation of African American males in out-of-school suspensions. Yet, the school's discipline system only required suspension for serious offenses or persistent discipline infractions. Concerned about why so many more African American males were being suspended, the principal decided to administer a survey to all students to gain insight on possible causes. The survey results showed that many students felt certain teachers were more likely than others to be overly punitive with regard to discipline procedures in general. African American males reported feeling that they did not belong. How did this school respond?

Actions taken

1. The principal looked closely at discipline referral data to determine which teachers were making the most referrals in order to confirm (or refute) the students' perceptions.

(Continued)

Table 2 (Continued)

2. In the event of a disproportionate number of referrals from certain teachers, the principal conducted individual teacher conferences to determine if there were additional supports or strategies that might be provided to the identified teachers. For example, the principal considered assigning a teacher mentor to assist with the implementation of the professional development strategies in the classroom.

3. All teachers were provided with professional development on classroom management and cultural competency.

4. To help African American males develop a sense of belonging in the school, the school leadership team implemented an in-school mentoring program in which students who had experienced more than one suspension were paired with a trained staff member who would greet the student each day, check homework, review expectations for the day, and set daily and weekly goals. The principal, school counselor, parent/guardian, and student also met to discuss a mentoring plan and outline expectations and parameters.

Source: Reproduced with permission from the Center for Comprehensive School Reform and Improvement (2009) p. 3.

But classroom climate, as created by the teacher, includes not only the emotional climate, but also pedagogy (teaching style, the type of curriculum) and disciplinary style (type of rules, how enforced, authoritativeness of the teacher, etc.) (Evans, Harvey, Buckley, & Yan, 2009). These three domains significantly interact. If students are interested in their work, feel secure rather than anxious, and are motivated to please their teacher, inappropriate behavior is likely to be at a minimum; teachers do not need to spend most of their time trying to maintain control. Similarly, if the teacher relies more on intrinsic and social rewards than external punishment and disapproval (a disciplinary style), motivation to learn and succeed is high, and the classroom has a positive emotional feel.

In other words, positive classroom climate both prevents the emergence of difficult behaviors that must be managed and provides the essential background whereby restorative discipline approaches can be implemented. And the key to classroom climate is the relationship between teacher and student—all students individually as well as the class as a whole. We know a great deal about how positive relationships can be fostered, and in the next sections we provide an overview of the issues that have sufficient research support to merit recommendation to practitioners.

Secondary Classrooms

We begin with the secondary school climate as this is the stage in the educational process when it is often assumed that teacher-student relationships become somewhat less important. Peer-group relationships predominate as teenagers struggle with role confusion and conflicting loyalties. Also, because each teacher may only see a particular class for one period a day, there is less opportunity to get to know students as individual personalities, and students in turn must negotiate the different demands and expectations of as many as six different subject teachers within just one school day. This also means that students can compare and contrast one teacher's style with that of another, making it harder for teachers to gain respect if they relate less effectively to teenagers.

The extent to which academic subjects are specialized also interacts with older high school students' abilities, interests, and career goals (general motivation). A student who sees a possible future as a professional surfer is more easily bored, inattentive, and disruptive during trigonometry than another who hopes to join the air force and be a pilot. Thus at the secondary level, emotional class climate is closely tied to (a) the relationship teachers have with students; (b) the degree to which values and emotional understanding are openly expressed and discussed in conversation (including when newsworthy topics of national and international interest are brought into the curriculum); (c) teachers' passions for the subject matter and their skill in exciting student interests; and (d) the respect that teachers show for students' abilities and potential.

Recent research highlights that older students like to be treated with respect. Middle school students want teachers "to show us that you like us and find us interesting" (Cushman & Rogers, 2008, p. 65). Of course the best way to find out interesting information about your teenage students is to ask them questions, listen, remember, and bring up the information received (unless private) in later conversations and in class. Many students happily reveal all sorts of things about themselves on their Facebook pages. The least constructive way to get interesting information about a student is to make it clear ahead of time that you don't like their choices in celebrities, music, clothes, tattoos, or body piercings.

Identifying and reducing risk for harm

Schools have in place various safety programs to reduce risk at the secondary level, including programs to deter bullying. By the time students are teenagers, threatening and risky behaviors can be quite hidden and adults may not even be aware of them, making it difficult, if not impossible, to manage those behaviors. When there is a positive emotional atmosphere, however, teachers hold young people to a high standard. They openly discuss issues and make their expectations clear. Rules and consequences are natural, fair, and applied firmly without fuss. A delicate balance needs to be maintained so that concerns about over-reacting to features of teenage lives that might appear deviant to adults do not interfere with responding to signs of emotional distress indicative of serious disorder. Peers are generally the best judges of the types of feelings that are out of the ordinary, which is why having brief class discussions of an issue the teacher is concerned about allows for different perspectives to be expressed. Teachers sometimes become aware of morbid and violent themes through adolescents' essays or artistic productions, although their seriousness is often hard to judge without probing further.

Classwide strategies

By talking with the class as a whole and avoiding a focus on any particular individual, the teacher can guide the discussion toward more reasoned judgments. Digital media create a whole new dimension for such concerns. An example is the private website set up by one of the two students responsible for the Columbine High School massacre: three years before the incident, the student blogged threats against other students and teachers at the school. While teachers who create a warm emotional climate are interested in ethnic and nationally derived cultural differences, they understand that the popular culture of the adolescent in Western societies often overshadows family traditions. They are aware of some of the more easily accessed pernicious websites on the Internet that can overly influence vulnerable young people who do not receive open, frank, and supportive guidance from parents.

As a practical procedure, emotionally competent teachers often use what they call the "CRC" technique (commend, recommend, commend again) defined by an intermediate school teacher as: *Always have two positives: first commend, then have a recommendation—not a criticism but a recommendation—and then have another second commendation to follow.* Finally, try to be alert to teachable moments that occur naturally in the classroom. For example, you should be alert to a shift in mood, a conflict, or a caring act. And remember to value social and emotional intelligence in your students as highly as you value their cognitive development.

An example: Abbas

These basic principles are illustrated in the following real-life example of a high school student who was a recent immigrant to the United States (see insert).

Abbas

Abbas had recently arrived from a Middle Eastern country to live with his uncle, who was an American citizen. Abbas, who was 15, was the oldest of eight siblings, the other seven of whom were living with his mother in Lebanon; his father had been killed in sectarian violence. Although his English was quite good, he was academically well behind his peers as he had had little exposure to the standard curriculum of Port Dickinson High. He was struggling in the ninth grade despite being older than all the others in the class. Although quiet and withdrawn at first, four months into school his behavior had become a significant concern. He had difficulty complying with school rules, was verbally and physically aggressive, consistently provoking peers by actions such as deliberately bumping into their desks, squirting water over them from the water bottle in his backpack, and deleting other students' work on the computer. He had been suspended three times by the end of that year, and the Deputy Principal was looking into finding an alternative school.

It was the beginning of the following year when his 10th-grade social studies teacher, Angelina Kane, noticed that although Abbas was described as a leading troublemaker, other students in the class were quick to make fun of him, openly referring to him as "abbas-hole," and ignoring him on the few occasions he did try to contribute in class. Angelina made a series of private appointments both with Abbas and his uncle, determined to get to know this student better. It became clear that he was accustomed to being the dominant influence back home in Beirut. He thought his peers were immature "children." He had conflict with his uncle's conversion to Christianity, yet he desperately wanted to be successful to make his mother proud of him. Although referred to the school counselor, he had refused to return after the first visit.

Angelina obtained from the uncle the name of an Islamic cultural center in Port Dickinson where a successful Lebanese-American businessman agreed to provide some mentoring. But it was what she set up in her social studies class that is most relevant to the present discussion. She initiated a weekly series of presentations by the students to explain their family backgrounds and ethnic-cultural origins, engineering it so that Abbas was about the third presenter. She set aside time for formal class discussions about name calling, teasing, provoking others, and consistently reminded the class of the school's values. She asked the class to generate some new principles that as a class they were going to try to implement that year—she thought some of them a bit unrealistic, but she wrote them up and e-mailed them or texted them to the class communication list. She explained quite openly that Abbas means "lion" in Arabic and was a name to be respected, not denigrated. She described the new "working teams" that she formed (avoiding any specific mention of friendships) in which every member of the team had to contribute to a new social studies project in which the goal was to generate a report on the national origins of the citizens of Port Dickinson, using old newspapers, historical records in the museum, or interviewing retired, lifelong residents of the town. And she asked Abbas's uncle (who was unmarried and had no children of his own) to seek counseling strictly for himself regarding parenting teenagers. By the end of 10th grade, Abbas was still no angel, but he had no suspensions, had made a few friends who enjoyed soccer rather than football, and regularly sought out Angelina for a chat at the end of the day.

Elementary Classrooms

The key ingredients that contribute to a positive, warm class climate in elementary school classrooms have a strong research base (Evans & Harvey, 2012):

1. First, the *relationship* between the teacher and every individual in the class must be warm and positive. This requires that all children are treated with equivalence. When talking to students in emotionally warm classrooms, the idea of being a family often comes up. Elementary students feel they can connect with teachers and communicate their feelings when teachers take the time to talk, stop whatever activities they were doing to actively listen, share information about themselves with students, display a congenial mood, and express positive regard and interest without lecturing. Students notice that if a warm teacher is too busy to address a concerned pupil's issues at that very moment, she or he will remember to come back to the topic later, ask the child to stop by for a chat at the end of the day, or find some other way of ensuring that expressed concerns are never dismissed or neglected. Elementary teachers may introduce a positive emotional climate in the classroom with something similar to a "question box," in which pupils can deposit questions on emotional and personal issues that have been concerning them. This type of system allows for discussions between teachers and elementary age students that cannot take place in class or publicly, for example, a discussion of socially awkward issues such as sexuality. Warmth, connection, caring, familiarity, emotional communication, and self-disclosure are themes that characterize positive emotional relationships between teachers and students in the Evans and Harvey (2012) research.

2. Second, teachers need to be *aware of their own emotions* as well as the emotions of their students. This requires a certain amount of self-reflection and willingness to analyze one's own feelings. Teachers actively put themselves in the "students' shoes" to understand their perspective and to be receptive to the students' emotional experiences. Awareness of the emotional environment allows teachers to prevent and defuse escalating conflict through altering emotional antecedents and consequences, or acting in a nonemotional manner to address the situation.

3. Third, it is necessary to have some philosophical ideas about the importance and the role of emotion. In the child development literature this is called *meta-emotion*: feelings about feelings. Teachers who create an emotionally warm climate see emotional expression

in children (and in themselves) as a "teachable moment"—an opportunity to talk to students about feelings.

4. Fourth, *emotion management* skills are required. Teachers need self-management strategies that allow them to cope with stressful situations, control anger and outbursts of temper, and to understand these strategies well enough that they can teach them to the students when the opportunity is right.

5. Finally, emotionally competent teachers have very clear *guidelines* about relationships and emotional situations. These include the importance of fairness, the establishment of consistent boundaries, rules, consequences, and predictable routines. Warnings are consistently followed through using low-key directives and minimal cues such as a look, a simple comment, and so on. Students feel safe if they have clear guidelines, limits, and boundaries, and know what to expect from a teacher.

Many hours observing elementary teachers with exemplary abilities in maintaining positive emotional climates in their classrooms taught us an important general atmosphere principle: these teachers rarely react in crisis mode when confronted with challenges. A good example of this was observed after a major fight during recess between a few boys in a particularly skilled teacher's class and some students from another classroom. After recess, the teacher busied himself with some (probably make-believe) task and then slowly, one by one, called over the four boys who had been involved in the altercation. Very quietly, he started a discussion with them. He listened patiently to each side of the story until they started blaming the other boys, and then he took a little more control. He said that who was to blame was not what he wanted to find out. What he wanted was for them to come up with a solution so the fighting would not be repeated.

This incident was extremely volatile but was managed calmly and effectively, after the students involved had calmed down. The teacher minimized their group cohesion by calling them up one by one until they were all sitting next to him. Some children, particularly those children with diagnoses such as autism (ASD) or severe conduct disorder, can exhibit major meltdowns—what some parents describe as "Richter-scale" tantrums. When these happen in class, it is key that the teacher help the child regain some self-regulation—going outside (not as punishment, as in so-called time out), taking a deep breath, even comforting and holding the student in extreme cases. There is no point in trying to introduce a plan when a child is totally out of control emotionally: remember the old adage that you cannot give swimming lessons to a drowning person.

An example: Disruption in third grade

The next example will sound familiar to teachers.

A Disruptive Third-Grade Classroom

Mrs. Dobbs expressed surprise that her class of third graders was constantly unruly and that she always had to raise her voice to obtain any degree of compliance with instructions. Mrs. Dobbs was an experienced teacher who had a reputation as a strict disciplinarian while achieving excellent academic results. This year, however, she found that she was making more and more threats, sending the two most disruptive boys out of the classroom almost daily, and having such a long list of small-scale punishments and negative consequences that she couldn't always remember what penalties she had already imposed. Becoming increasingly frustrated, she spoke to the teacher who taught the class the previous year, a recent graduate named Ms. Williamson, about her problems with the class. Ms. Williamson was surprised—she agreed that the class was a spirited bunch but they had always seemed eager to learn and enjoy a good laugh. Mrs. Dobbs admitted that she never laughed, then disclosed that she was actually terribly tense and was having difficulty managing her temper because her teenage son was being treated for cancer. Ms. Williamson suggested that Mrs. Dobbs talk to her class about this, but Mrs. Dobbs was reluctant, dismissing it as inappropriate to bring her personal issues into class.

A week later, after a series of very difficult incidents with the two naughtiest boys, she actually broke down in class and had to leave in tears. She returned with Ms. Williamson in support, and she explained to the stunned and now totally silent class that she was experiencing major stresses because of family illness. She apologized for her grouchy behavior. She didn't go into the full details about her son's medical condition, but one of the girls in the class volunteered that there was a lot of tension in her own home because her brother had been in a serious accident. Another girl talked about how her mom practiced yoga to stay calm after a hard day as a store assistant. The next few days, whenever there was spare time, class discussion revolved around stress, how to cope, how not to sweat the small annoyances. One of the boys who had been regularly sent out of the room for behavior told a fairly silly joke he had heard from his dad. Mrs. Dobbs and the whole class laughed. Mrs. Dobbs said she wanted a new joke every Friday morning—some were so poor she later regretted this decision, but her mood was substantially better and the class atmosphere became more positive. The class, on their own initiative, all signed a get-well card for Mrs. Dobbs's son.

School Climate as the Context for Classroom Climate

Although we have been focusing this discussion on the climate that you as a teacher can promote in individual classrooms, we recognize that it is very difficult to create emotionally sensitive teaching contexts unless the majority of the school community is firmly committed to a positive schoolwide climate. In the United States, the National School Climate Center (NSCC), founded by Jonathan Cohen, has proposed five standards that define an effective school climate (Cohen, 2006):

1. Plans or a vision for promoting and sustaining a positive school climate (discussions across the school led by the principal)

2. Practices that enhance engagement in learning and schoolwide activities are prioritized

3. Policies promote social, emotional, civic, and intellectual skills and address barriers to learning and teaching

4. Members of the school community are welcomed, supported, and feel safe

5. Students and teachers engage in practices that promote responsibility and social justice

Consider the word choices used in these broad standards. "Engagement" in learning and school activities is crucial for positive, restorative, disciplinary methods. "Social, emotional, civic, and intellectual skills" conveys one of Cohen's most important ideas—that it is through experiencing school as a community teaching conscientiousness and values—that citizens of the future learn civic responsibility and democracy. That students (and teachers) should feel "welcomed, supported, and safe" emphasizes how important it is that all students feel they belong—that they are connected to the school so that disciplinary methods never incorporate exclusion or rejection. Finally, "social responsibilities and social justice" are words that capture the very essence of restorative methods.

In addition to those general standards, the NSCC has a useful checklist of specific indicators of positive school climate that can be used as a checklist for your own practice. NSCC checklist items reflect indicators such as "Every student is connected to a caring and responsible adult in the school" and "School, family, and youth members collaboratively develop . . . codes of conduct that support positive and sustained school climate." Collecting and reporting data by using checklists such as these allow school personnel and teachers to evaluate whether their initiatives already in place are actually having the desired effects. If you are not a person who likes checklists, you can instead ask small focus groups of students simply to discuss their impressions of the school climate. The Minneapolis Public School system has a freely available toolkit entitled *Creating a Positive School Climate for Learning* (see http://sss.mpls.k12.mn.us/Positive_School_Climate_Tool_Kit.html). The Minneapolis group recommends that focus groups of representative students could be asked the following questions to evaluate how things are going:

- How do you feel when you come to this school?
- If you don't know what to do in the classroom, whom do you ask?
- Do you feel safe on the bus ride/walk to this school?
- What would you like to change about this school?
- How is your family involved with this school? In your education?

TEACHING STYLES

This section addresses the issue of teacher or teaching styles, particularly with reference to how the teacher's approach to learning and behavior can have an impact on both individual student behavior and the classroom's group behavior. For example, Kleinfeld's (1975) description of the "warm demander" refers to a style considered to characterize an effective teacher. This style contrasts with a teacher whose positive relationships with students seem to be supported primarily by being an "easy teacher" who does not expect a great deal from students, thus ironically encouraging low achievement. It also contrasts with teachers who have a reputation for requiring students to perform at a high level that may be at the expense of caring for students, and may involve ignoring the appropriate level of challenge for at least some students. More sophisticated taxonomies of teacher characteristics have recently been developed (see below), but this early concept of warm demanders was useful in creating awareness of the need for teachers to achieve a balance between having positive relationships with students while still holding high expectations.

Teachers can demonstrate a far broader range of effective styles, as described by Wubbels and Brekelmans' (2005) *dimensional* model of interpersonal teacher behavior. Their model parallels the well-established dimensions of successful parenting (Baumrind, 1991), as well as sharing similarities with effective psychotherapy and counseling practices (Lonner, 1980). One dimension represents dominance versus submission; the dominant teacher determines the student's activities (much like a "demander") whereas at the submissive end, the students can determine their own activities. Although you as a teacher may tend towards one of these dimensional extremes, your dominance will also *vary* from day to day, class to class, according to the type of lesson, the subject matter, and to some extent the personalities of the students you are teaching. The second dimension is labeled cooperation versus opposition. Cooperation is characterized by showing approval of the students and their behavior (similar to being "warm"), and opposition is characterized by showing disapproval.

Now, if you think of these two dimensions forming a cross, at right angles to each other, you will see that the quadrants describe interaction styles. For parents, Maccoby and Martin (1983) feature the dimensions of demanding (dominance) to undemanding and responsive (cooperation) to unresponsive, which are four styles usually described as:

1. *Authoritarian*: young people are expected to follow strict rules established by their parents. Children raised this way may be obedient but less likely to be happy and have lower self-esteem.

2. *Authoritative*: authoritative parents have rules usually mutually agreed upon; they are responsive to their children and tend to forgive rather than punish. Children reared this way tend to be happy and successful.

3. *Permissive*: indulgent parents make few demands on their children; they allow self-regulation rather than mature behavior. They may be nurturing and communicative but avoid confrontation, and the children often have difficulty with authority and do not perform at school as well as they could academically.

4. *Uninvolved*: these parents make few demands, are unresponsive and uncommunicative; in more extreme cases they may be rejecting and neglectful. Their children have low self-esteem and are less likely to develop high levels of social or academic competence.

In the analysis of teacher styles proposed by Wubbels and Brekelmans (2005), each of these general quadrants can be divided in two, depending on which dimension a style most closely represents. So, for example, teachers who are very high on the characteristic of "opposition" but only fairly high on "dominance" might tend to have rules focused on what not to do, may get angry easily, take pupils to task, express irritation, and emphasize correcting behavior followed by negative consequences. This is the opposite of a restorative ethos. Teachers who are very high on "cooperation" and fairly high on "submission" might tend to listen with interest, be confident and understanding, accept apologies, look for ways to settle differences, and be open and patient. Teachers very high on dominance and fairly high on cooperation might be good leaders and organizers, likely to set tasks and determine procedures, structure the classroom well, explain things, and hold the attention of the students.

With the exception of extreme cases falling into one or another quadrant, these different styles cannot really be identified as right or wrong, good or bad. They will reflect the personality of the teacher, what the teacher is comfortable with, and may change considerably according to teacher mood, the mood of the class, and the type of instruction. Also, depending on the personality of each student, the group composition of the class, and the student's parenting experience and cultural expectations, some of these teacher styles will fit better with certain individuals than with others. While the "warm demander" concept suggests a useful way of thinking about the balance between caring for students as culturally located individuals and having high expectations, a more complex dimensional model also supports the words of Mark Twain that "there is more than one way to skin a cat!"

CULTURALLY RESPONSIVE RELATIONSHIPS

School traditions and practices can devalue and even visibly exclude the heritage, culture, and language of other student populations—students who represent Indigenous, African American, Hispanic, and many different immigrant peoples (Alton-Lee, 2003; Bishop, 2011). Mainstream schools often reflect a dominant culture that is typically invisible to persons in authority and to students from that culture, who sometimes even insist that the school context is "culture-free" or represents universal values (we would argue that neither of these is actually possible). Essentially, an invisible dominant culture privileges those students who share the dominant cultural identity and disadvantages those students whose cultures are different. Schools are seldom "multicultural" despite goal statements to that effect, but implicitly assert dominant cultural values that bypass minority cultural values—through their organizational structures, language, materials, and symbolism that provide the systemic context for affirming some cultural identities and devaluing others.

Because the classroom is the daily lived experience of students, how the classroom either does or does not validate students' cultural identities and cultural knowledge can have a profound impact on student outcomes (Gutiérrez & Rogoff, 2003; Sleeter & Grant, 2009). In the absence of culturally responsive practices, where there is a lack of connection between the culture of the school and that of the students and their families, the result will be a lack of motivation and engagement (Castagno & Brayboy, 2008). For students from nondominant cultural groups, low expectations and student alienation often play out through high suspension rates, over representation in special education, low educational attainment, and higher dropout rates than for students from the dominant culture (Gilborn, 2008). Traditional educational solutions to disparities fail to acknowledge the possibility of systemic discrimination; instead, disproportionate representation of "minority" students in remedial and special education is a direct reflection of deficit theorizing explanations that locate the problem in students and their families.

Culturally Responsive Authentic Caring

Valenzuela (1999) describes the difference between aesthetic caring that involves sharing affective expressions with children and authentic caring that entails deep reciprocity. Authentic caring for teachers means taking responsibility—assuming "agency"—for providing an education environment in which students can thrive. Authentic caring requires the teacher to get to know students well, to invite student input regarding teaching and learning activities in the classroom, to respect students' intellectual abilities, and to demonstrate valuing identities that students bring into school from home by incorporating aspects of their identity in how the curriculum is presented and assessed. Another way to describe authentic caring is "caring for students as culturally located individuals," which, again, goes beyond simple feelings to implications for teacher pedagogy and how teachers support student learning (Bishop, 2011).

Kleinfeld's (1975) original work on the concept of warm demanders described effective teachers of indigenous students who demonstrated authentic caring. These teachers genuinely cared for their students and established a warm classroom climate, but also insisted that students meet academic goals and do their work (Irvine, 2003; Ross, Bondy, Gallingane, & Hambacher, 2008). Teachers try to achieve a balance between supporting and caring for students while also requiring students to stretch themselves academically. Effective teachers set high expectations for students that are challenging for them but within their grasp if they do the work, hence firmly but warmly demand that students meet those expectations and do not accept excuses, disengagement, or task avoidance in their classroom.

Ware's (2006) research on culturally responsive teaching investigated unique and culturally specific teaching styles that contribute to achievement in African American and other children of color. She identified African American teachers who were effective:

- **Ms. Willis,** working in an urban elementary school in the district's lowest socioeconomic region, taught students from Grades 3 to 5 who had behavioral problems or were underachieving but not in special education. She had a "tough-minded, no-nonsense style of teaching" and spoke to students in a loud clear voice; when she spoke, students were absolutely quiet and there were no movements or nonverbal gestures indicating anything other than respect. She was particularly insistent about homework being completed on time and while she acknowledged that students did not always control aspects of their lives, she accepted no excuses for not doing one's work.

- **Mrs. Carter** taught middle school students at a recently renovated school designed to feature technology and attract middle-income as well as low-income families. Despite a range of abilities in her classes, she expected all the students to achieve academically and did not accept poverty as an excuse for not meeting achievement goals. Her high expectations are evident in the following quote: "Good job Johnny—you did this, now, go back and add four more steps to it and make it even better" (p. 447). Her use of "mean talk" was described as showing caring alongside authoritative explicit explanations of expecting more from the students. She emphasized that because the students were accustomed to certain responses, for example "if you don't give them that response they will read that as weakness . . . 'I can do this and she won't even say anything to me' whereas if the teacher responds immediately, there will be no problem" (Ware, 2006, p. 438). A teacher's cultural background will not match every student's, nor is this necessary. Research on authentic caring highlights behaviors and expectations exhibited by culturally sensitive and pedagogically responsive teachers who have developed particular skills and understandings. These are within the grasp of any teacher willing to work on being more effective with not just the self-starters and high-achieving students, but with those who present challenges and have not done well in school in the past.

Culturally Responsive Pedagogies

Gay (2010) defines culturally responsive pedagogy as teaching "to and through [students'] personal and cultural strengths, their intellectual capabilities, and their prior accomplishments" (p. 26) and as premised on "close interactions among ethnic identity, cultural background, and student achievement" (p. 27). Conceptually, culturally responsive pedagogy also aligns well with the promotion of teaching that acknowledges the multiple "funds of knowledge" that students bring to the classroom (Gonzalez, Moll, & Amanti, 2005). The funds of knowledge perspective appreciate that students bring diverse valued identities to the classroom from their families and communities (e.g., culture, views of self, family values), requiring that teachers get to know their students pedagogically. Gonzalez et al. explain that if learning is to be maximized for students, both teachers and schools must incorporate those funds of knowledge in curricula and as part of learning activities. Culturally responsive teachers accept the challenge to contextualize instruction in cultural forms, behaviors, and processes of learning familiar to students. Books by Gay (2010) and Sleeter (2011) provide professional educators with a solid framework for understanding the importance of being culturally responsive as well as validated exemplars translating good intentions into actual classroom teaching and learning practices.

A particularly strong example of embedding culturally responsive pedagogies into classrooms well and long enough to affect students is Cammarota and Romero's (2009) case study of secondary Hispanic students in high-poverty schools in Tucson, Arizona. The program is based on a model of intellectually challenging content and culturally responsive pedagogy with a strong foundation of positive relationships between teachers and students. They were able to show that student participation in the program had a positive impact on their subsequent academic achievement.

Another initiative that demonstrated the positive impact of culturally responsive pedagogies on student learning and behavior is the *Te Kotahitanga* teacher professional development program implemented throughout New Zealand (Bishop, 2011; Sleeter, 2011). Teachers learn culturally responsive pedagogies for teaching indigenous Maori students attending mainstream secondary schools, based on an "effective teaching profile (ETP)" that is grounded in student narratives about what students want from their teachers. The ETP requires that teachers assume agency (i.e., as a teacher, I can make a difference for this child) for enhancing student outcomes rather than adopting deficit theories to explain failure (e.g., the student refuses to learn, the family is dysfunctional, etc.) and incorporates the following dimensions:

- Developing positive relationships with students as learners
- Caring for students as culturally located individuals
- Using discursive teaching and learning approaches
- Incorporating a range of teaching strategies to facilitate learning interactions
- Having high expectations for students
- Promoting, monitoring, and reflecting learning outcomes with students
- Managing the class to promote learning

Some of these dimensions are associated with good teaching generally; others are specific to being culturally responsive. Multiple examples are provided in Sleeter (2011), including evidence of the positive impact of this teacher professional development on schools, teachers, families, school personnel generally, and the students themselves—indigenous as well as all students in schools. The principles and approaches to effective pedagogies have been described in sufficient detail to allow adaptation and replication to address similar kinds of cultural mismatches among schools, teachers, and students in other countries (Berryman, 2011; Hindle et al., 2011).

SUMMARY

This chapter provides an overview of principles for enhancing classroom climate along with specific examples of how to establish a warm classroom climate at elementary and secondary levels. The chapter also discusses different teaching styles, along with the need for teachers who are culturally aware and who use culturally responsive practices with students. Teachers may be called on to develop new skills and understandings so that they can ensure positive relationships with students from diverse cultural and linguistic backgrounds that may differ from the dominant school culture. The content of the chapter provides an overview of regular education practices that benefit all students in creating the foundation for positive learning and behavior. Next, Chapter 5 develops specific strategies that teachers can adapt and apply in regular classrooms that meet the needs of most students and that should be in place prior to referrals for the individualized interventions covered in Chapters 6 and 7.

5 School and Classroom Support Structures

T his chapter covers processes to establish a community of learners in the classroom, including cooperative learning and peer support networks whereby students support one another's learning. Ongoing approaches for problem solving by children are described along with examples of how teachers can engage students actively to address challenges. The chapter also describes practices for the prevention and peaceful resolution of conflict based on a restorative ethos that guides everything within the school. Restorative practices and restorative curricula across grades are described, including restorative language and scripts, restorative inquiry, restorative conversations, and use of meetings and conferences. Mediation, shuttle mediation, and peer mediation are introduced, along with the processes involved in formal conferences for serious offenses as part of a restorative school discipline framework. Combined with Chapter 4, this chapter covers the basic elements of positive approaches in regular classrooms that are the foundation for the design of individualized interventions covered in Chapters 6 and 7.

COMMUNITY AND PEER SUPPORT IN CLASSROOMS

School is obviously the place where children cumulatively master the academic material and cognitive skills needed for future lives as well-educated citizens who support themselves and their families, work, and contribute to society. There is also a larger view of the purpose of schooling that acknowledges as educational outcomes a range of noncognitive skills that can be just as important for later learning and employment outcomes (Covay & Carbonaro, 2010). For students, classrooms are social and emotional as well as educational places: school may be the first significant opportunity for many children to learn how to interact socially as part of a wider community outside the family. Being in school means intensive and extensive relationships with not just teachers and other adults but also with other children and youth—their peers. Young people do form social relationships with peers outside school through family and neighborhood connections, but most students develop peer relationships and friendships that started as interactions in school, in the classroom, on the playground, and in school extracurricular activities. Thus, what happens to children in your classroom plays a critical role in their social lives and can even determine whether or not they develop friendships and the capacity to evidence emotions such as empathy and kindness. The impact of classrooms on children's social-emotional lives is an important reason for teachers to consider how their own actions affect the social structure of the classroom.

Furthermore, without intervention, classrooms are *invisible* social structures that can either hinder or facilitate teaching and learning processes. If, for example, unbeknownst to the teacher, subtle exclusion and even bullying behavior is happening during class, individual students can be exposed continuously to hostile learning experiences. When students are allowed or even invited to sit where they wish, the classroom can also reinforce "cliques" that represent social hierarchies in school—creating a social network that formalizes who's in versus who's out, causing anxiety and embarrassment for children who are seldom selected. In addition, enabling students who have varied behavioral challenges to sit together is also inviting trouble. Teachers increase behavior management issues geometrically with student seating arrangements that can actually encourage rather than prevent contagion and mutually negative influences within student groups.

It is important for teachers to recognize the social nature of the classroom and break down the hypothetical large group of 25 to 35 students into manageable and socially supportive small groups. The development of positive skills for working with other students across the school years is a key goal in schools committed to restorative practices. Cooperative learning is a well-researched approach that provides a solid foundation for the development of positive networks and social interaction skills in the classroom, but also extends beyond into children's lives outside school and in the future. Teachers use varied instructional formats such as individual seatwork, whole-class instruction, and discussion groups in the classroom. In addition, use of cooperative learning strategies enables children to master both academic material and interpersonal skills. Engaging your class in cooperative learning for at least some portion of their day has been shown to enhance achievement, social skills, and prosocial behaviors. Cooperative learning also builds classroom cultures so that when challenges occur, students have the skills and emotional understanding for restorative practices (Roseth, Johnson, & Johnson, 2008).

Cooperative Learning Structures

Simply putting students into groups for activities in the classroom is *not* cooperative learning—cooperative learning is a complex process that involves more than telling students to work cooperatively with one another. Putnam (1998) has helpfully listed the essential components of cooperative learning that distinguish it from traditional group instruction:

- *Positive interdependence:* All members of the group work together and coordinate the contributions of each student's individual goal as well as that of the final group goal. Success requires that students tutor one another and check on one another's progress.
- *Individual accountability:* Each student in the group is individually responsible for mastering the learning outcome and making a contribution to the group outcome, with no "hitchhikers" riding along while other members of the group do most of the work. Each student may be required to monitor themselves by filling out an individual report about contributions to the group, reaching individual learning goals, accomplishments, and how to improve his or her accountability.
- *Cooperative skills taught directly:* Students learn and practice age-appropriate social and cooperative skills within the group, with roles assigned and feedback provided on how well each student is using the skill. Elementary students might practice sharing materials, taking turns, and speaking in classroom voices, whereas secondary students might work on active listening, paraphrasing one another, and resolving disagreements by discussing ideas rather than criticizing persons.
- *Face-to-face interaction:* The task should be one in which students actively interact with one another, not simply work side-by-side independently. It is not cooperative learning if students discuss their answers with one another after working out those answers independently: this is what Johnson, Johnson, and Holubec (1990) referred to as individualistic learning with talking.

- *Student reflection and goal setting:* When the cooperative learning activity is finished, students evaluate how well they've done working together as a group both academically and socially. This can be done within groups or across the entire class after group work. Both the teacher and students themselves set social and cooperative goals for the next cooperative activity based on this evaluation.
- *Heterogeneous groups:* A key principle in cooperative learning is that the small groups are heterogeneous. Tracked, streamed, or ability groups, by definition, violate a fundamental principle of cooperative learning. This is because one of the key underlying values of cooperative learning is for students to learn to work with others across differences, strengths, and weaknesses. This does not mean that groups cannot be organized by interest area (e.g., for a project) or a component of a task (e.g., as in jigsaw groups where groups work on different aspects then come together for the final product), but it does require that each group represent a mixture of cognitive abilities, achievement levels, social and behavioral skills, genders, socioeconomic levels, cultural identities, and language characteristics. Equal opportunity for success: Each student should have the opportunity to contribute meaningfully to reaching the group goal, which may require individualized criteria for success and modifications to task requirements appropriate for strengths and needs.

Thus, cooperative learning is not a structure allowing the teacher to withdraw from the instructional process and leave students to fend for their own learning by "putting students into groups." Instead, the teacher actively observes and monitors how groups are going, and the teacher provides regular feedback to the class about the development of cooperative skills as well as academic outcomes. One of the challenges teachers face when implementing cooperative learning is that students may have been put into groups for various classroom activities on numerous occasions in previous years, but these were not structured cooperative learning groups. This means that students may actually have to unlearn expectations about which kinds of groups they will have (expecting to work only with their friends or only those on the same ability level, for example) or how they will work together (where some students take on most of the work and others are passive, doing little in the group, for example). Teachers may have experience with doing "group work" which they believe was a form of cooperative learning, hence will say something like "I tried cooperative learning once, but it simply doesn't work with this age group." The fact is that there is strong empirical support for the effectiveness of well-designed cooperative learning structures across all ages (Roseth, Johnson, & Johnson, 2008).

There are many texts and manuals available to train teachers with the basics of cooperative learning. Cooperative learning is likely to have been addressed in preservice teacher education programs, and many districts and schools regularly provide opportunities for inservice teachers to receive training in its use. However, in this guide, we address the issue of how to group students for learning activities in the classroom. Just as children haven't yet mastered all academic content skills, it is safe to assume that they initially lack the crucial interpersonal skills needed to work collaboratively in small groups and support one another academically and socially. For Restorative Classroom Discipline to be a reality, the classroom must be a safe place where children feel cared for and supported. If children know how to help and cooperate with one another, they will have mastered essential life skills that they need in adult life at work, at home, in the community, and in all their interpersonal relationships. Small groups in the classroom can be an important social context for mastering prosocial skills and emotion knowledge. Hence, the next section describes empirically established strategies for structuring heterogeneous groups that promote both learning and positive social behavior.

Constructing Peer Support Networks

Students are seated for their classroom work in different patterns that vary according to teacher preferences, student preferences, subject area, classroom size, and the nature of activities. Furthermore, these seating arrangements must also accommodate different instructional formats such as whole class, independent seatwork, and working in pairs or groups. Students may be assigned seats by the teacher (typical in elementary school) or allowed to sit where they like (more usual at middle and secondary schools). When they sit where they like, students are also likely to choose to sit semipermanently in small social clusters with friends; in turn, these seating clusters can exclude students who have no friends in that class because they are new, rejected, or socially isolated. Student seating clusters may be prosocial wherein so-called good students encourage and support one another. Student seating may also be seen as directly leading to behavioral management challenges where clusters of students with behavioral challenges sit together or individual students who are aggressive are seated in an area where they may be even more disruptive (e.g., at the back of the room or next to students who can become "victims"). Hence, seating arrangements are a major building block in the establishment of positive social structures in the classroom.

Teachers make one of two choices at the start of the year or semester, either allowing students to sit where they like or organizing seating in some way. In either case, we advocate that teachers announce that these seating arrangements are temporary and will be changed after a brief start-up period of perhaps 1 to 2 weeks while the teacher establishes new seating patterns to accommodate the work of the classroom. Ideally, seating arrangements should facilitate easy movement across different instructional formats so that, for example, cooperative learning group members are seated near one another to move swiftly into that mode. Planning seating arrangements and cooperative learning subgroups has a major impact on the nature of social interactions in your classroom and also helps to develop children's social skills and friendships. Without planning, seating arrangements exacerbate existing social inequities and behavioral challenges.

Teachers do not have a great deal of information about their students early in the school year, including school interests, academic achievement, and peer interaction patterns. Waiting for this knowledge to develop indirectly through classroom exposure may take weeks, and teachers should prepare the social context of their classrooms as soon as possible. To do this, we've adapted cooperative learning to accommodate other relevant child characteristics beyond the usual recommendation that groups be 'heterogeneous' so that each cooperative group—and cluster of seating arrangements—also has the capacity to function as a peer support network (Fisher, Bernazzani, & Meyer, 1998). The model requires the teacher to carry out an informal assessment of children's interests and preferences as one of the first activities in the classroom, and the information you gain from these assessments contributes to assignment of desks and to putting groups together for work in class.

Table 3 includes the usual criteria for constructing cooperative learning groups in different curricular areas, which is augmented by additional criteria to plan peer support networks. These additional criteria were developed by Meyer and Henry (1993) to specify planned groupings of children who can support one another and potentially develop friendships. To construct the groups, the teacher administers a brief Student Interest Inventory. The teacher tells the children that the answers to the questions will help the teacher make seating assignments for working in groups.

Figures 1 and 2 illustrate sample inventories adapted for elementary and secondary age students, respectively, and for very young children (e.g., kindergarten to Grades 1–2). Teachers will need to do the inventory as individual interviews that can be done during typical classroom activities across a period of a day or two. Teachers are familiar enough with the age group that they teach as well as their community context to design appropriate adaptations to these inventories. Have the inventory ready for the first class meeting and explain to the students that its purpose is to make seating and group work assignments that will be set up within a

Table 3 Criteria for Constructing Peer Support Networks

General criteria for cooperative learning groups

Each group is heterogeneous with respect to:

Gender

Ethnicity (e.g., Hispanic, African American, European American, Native American)

Subject area achievement level

Ability

Learning preferences (e.g., independent, group)

Specific criteria for peer support networks

Only one "at-risk" student per group

If possible, groups with an English as a second language (ESL) student should also include a student who is bilingual with the same first language but more fluent in English

Avoid risky combinations per group such as putting a bully with a victim; more than one off-task student; more than one potentially explosive student

Position one "worker" and/or "diplomat/peace-keeper" in each group

Building specific peer supports

For each group with an at-risk student, select one to two students who might be a potential friend who:

Can be a good influence or role model

Have similar interests and hobbies

Are of similar academic ability (but doing better academically and/or having better attendance records)

Seem to be good personality matches with the at-risk student (how to judge? Use your observation or best guess)

In addition, for each group of four students, include one mutual choice if possible (students who named one another on their inventories) and at least one student who was not named by any of the other three in the group

---

Source: Adapted with permission from Meyer and Henry (1993).

week or so. Tell students that the first couple of weeks with the new seating arrangement are on a trial basis and that students can talk with you privately about any changes that they feel are needed.

In constructing your seating arrangements and groups, follow the criteria listed in Table 3. You'll use the results of the interest inventory to construct pairs, combining two pairs to form groups of four, and two groups of four to groups of eight for seat and desk assignments in the

Figure 1 Student Interest Inventory for Elementary School

What is your favorite center/subject?

What do you like to do in school?

What don't you like to do in school?

What things do you like to play with outside school?

What do you like to do at home?

What is your favorite story? What is it about?

What is your favorite movie/TV show?

Whom do you want to sit next to? (name 3)

Whom do you want to play with at recess? (name 3)

Source: Adapted with permission from Meyer and Fisher (1999).

Figure 2 Student Interest Inventory for Middle and High School

What is your favorite subject?

What subject do you prefer the least?

What kinds of assignments do you like best? Least?

What is your favorite movie or television program?

Whose music do you like best? (name 3 bands or individuals)

What is your favorite social network or website?

What is your favorite videogame?

What sport do you like best? To do or to watch?

What extracurricular activity do you like?

Do you have a job outside school? If so, what is it?

Whom do you want to sit next to in this class? (name 3)

Whom would you pick to work with you for a group assignment? (name 3)

Source: Adapted with permission from Meyer and Fisher (1999).

room. Forming these peer support networks is a bit like a "dating service" in that the teacher is attempting to put students together in seating and working groups who discover they have things in common and can learn to work well together. Being systematic in this way also supports the development of new friendships that might never grow and flourish if students simply stayed with their existing friends; these networks can also break down negative peer relationships and establish opportunities for isolated children to become socially included. Be transparent with the children in making it clear that they will be seated together with at least one person they named as someone they like but will also be seated near people they have not named: Tell the children that this is deliberate because in life we often must work with lots of different people so doing this in the classroom is a starting point and will also allow new friendships to emerge.

Where there are difficulties within pairs and groups after 1 to 2 weeks of working together, it is important to resolve these difficulties and make changes to groups without recrimination and any appearance that some children are being rejected. Tell students to write you a note privately by a certain date if they are having any difficulties and wish to request a change in seating assignment, and you can then use this cumulative information to make any and all changes to seating assignments on one date rather than seeming to target a particular group or child.

Once student pairs and groups with respective seating and work station assignments have been made, the context exists for students to work together on tasks from across the curriculum. Teachers who employ cooperative learning in the classroom need to examine academic content on a regular basis to identify opportunities for children to practice interdependent learning rather than simply working side-by-side or completely independently. Figure 3 shows a sample classroom activity for first grade that requires two children to work together towards solving a problem yet ensuring that each child must take responsibility for completing the activity and practicing art skills. Similar lessons can be developed across the curriculum and across different ages—almost anything can be redesigned as a joint activity to be completed by two or more students rather than by individuals in the classroom.

The student pairs and groups that you establish in the classroom for academic activities provide a safe framework for students to practice their social skills and learn to problem solve disagreements and conflict. Tell your students that in your classroom, the focus on mastering subject content is important and, in addition, classroom citizenship is also important. You have already explained how you put the groups together

Figure 3 Group Lesson in Art for First-Grade Students

Goal:	Arts and intercultural education.
Objective:	How can we design a pair of mittens?
Materials:	Mitten cutouts for each child and color markers or crayons.
Motivation:	Read the story *The Mitten*, a Ukrainian folktale. What did the boy lose in the woods? What happened to his mitten?
Procedure:	Explain to the children that because the boy's mitten was destroyed by the animals, we will design a new pair of mittens for him. With the whole class, brainstorm colors and designs that might be on the mittens. Give each child a mitten cutout of paper, with each child pair receiving right and left. Tell the children they will work with their partner to make a pair of mittens. Define a pair as two mittens that match, right and left. They must work together so that each child creates a mitten that is a mirror image of his or her partner's mitten.
Follow-up:	Create a display of mittens entitled "Can you find a pair?"

Source: Designed by Alex Umbria and Nachum Winkler and reprinted with permission from Meyer and Fisher (1999).

using their answers to the interest inventory, and students should hear the general message that:

"We help one another to succeed in this classroom. When there is something challenging to learn and when there are disagreements, we have to learn how to problem solve together to come up with solutions. That means we will be spending time working on learning how to cooperate and help one another just as we are spending time learning mathematics, reading, and so on."

A consistent message in the class should be that if problems arise that cannot be solved by the group, groups might change but no one will be isolated from a group as a strategy to solve a problem.

Ongoing Group Problem-Solving Processes

In our work in schools, we observed teachers using diverse approaches to conducting problem-solving sessions with their students. In one elementary school classroom in New York City, the teacher created a small group "tea time" at a special table in the room where each group met separately with the teacher once a week to talk about an issue. A second teacher at that same school used a weekly classroom meeting in which agenda items were identified by the teacher and students, while a third teacher defined the "roundtable" as the place for pairs who had serious problems to meet with the teacher for work on communication skills. As a general practice, all teachers should utilize impromptu group meetings as needed presenting hypothetical problems for discussion by the students—for example, this can be based on teacher knowledge of an issue, or an anecdote that is circulating around the school about a problem that has arisen.

Young children require several lessons before they become comfortable with discussions about problems and start to learn how to reach agreement on who could do what to solve a problem. Older students present other challenges, as they undoubtedly harbor strong feelings and have definite opinions about issues that may interfere with hearing multiple perspectives. The key principle is, however, to bring these issues to the classroom in an open and transparent way rather than ignoring them or sweeping them under the rug (by not mentioning a problem and assuming that it has gone away because it isn't being discussed). In our experience, the combination of systematic planning for seating and group work arrangements alongside an ongoing mechanism for group problem solving has a dramatic impact on classroom management, with teachers reporting that up to 90 percent of their discipline events literally disappeared with the implementation of these practices.

Collaborative Problem Solving

Fairy tales, children's literature, and rhymes often contain kernels of truth that describe common problems and challenges while reflecting societal attitudes. Laments about unfairness are common—from adults and children alike—at different times in our lives. Perceptions of fairness and unfairness pervade cultural values and mores across nations, coming quite close to what might be considered a universal feature of judgments about human interactions, consequences, and social structures (Bierhoff, Cohen, & Greenberg, 1986). Social justice judgments pervade government policies and economics in the allocation of resources, and much social policy has its roots in philosophical theories about justice. Taxation policies in many countries internationally represent a kind of redistribution following the principle "from each according to ability; to each according to need." Decisions about whether elementary age children who speak Spanish as their first language should be taught basic skills in their first language or in English is debated according to beliefs about whether it is fair to make these kinds of accommodations for some students while other students are expected to learn without instruction in *their* first language or dialect. Ideas about fairness pervade international relations as well: should the families of student victims of an earthquake who were studying in another country be compensated differently from the families of citizens of that country who were also victims? Which country is responsible for compensation when a *force majeure* results in harm or death—the host or origin country? Complex issues are involved in such discussions, and the development of ideas about fairness can have a profound influence on one's adjustment and reaction to future events, relationships with others, and overall well-being.

Children have their first exposure to ideas about fairness in their families, perhaps thinking that a punishment was unfair or that a sibling was given a privilege that is unfair. School and classrooms play a major role in the development of ideas about fairness, including whether as a general rule, children mature thinking that society at large is fair or unfair to them. Evans, Goldberg-Arnold, and Dickson (1998) describe how children react to situations that provoke "fairness judgments" that are almost second nature to people. Without intervention, such judgments can create obstacles for and undermine accommodations needed for children experiencing difficulties who are not "ready" to do exactly what is expected of other children. Later in this guide, we describe the intervention planning process for children whose challenges are quite significant and who must be given time and opportunity to grow their capacity to master new skills and understandings. Children with disabilities, for example, may take longer and need more support than typical children at the same age level and in the same classroom. If accommodations designed to meet their needs create perceptions of "unfairness" in other children (and even adults) because they seem to violate rules others are expected to follow, these perceptions can become additional obstacles that interfere with social acceptance and support. How then can we accommodate differences without feeling that standards are being violated and that someone or some action is unfair?

To address these responses based on ideas about fairness, Salisbury, Evans, and Palombaro (1997) introduced an intervention they labeled *collaborative problem solving*. Collaborative problem solving is designed to combat subtle forms of discrimination and resentment directed towards adaptations and accommodations made for students with significant disabilities according to their individualized programs in regular classrooms. Consider what might happen when students in a class are given a worksheet to complete with a large number of problems as part of their seatwork in mathematics. In this same class at the same time, a student diagnosed as having a learning disability and attention deficit hyperactivity disorder (ADHD) might be given a worksheet with only half as many problems—equally challenging for him but doable and adjusted appropriately to meet his needs. That child's classmates (and other teachers) might consider this modification to be unfair and even argue that unless and until that student can do the same work as the other students he has no right to be in the classroom. Evans and his colleagues have shown that, in fact, children are quite capable of seeing such adjustments, accommodations, and modifications as fair if the reasons for these are explained to them and if they can see that the student whose work is different is also being expected to meet goals. Thus, having different goals and adjustments to curricula do not signal that a child cannot be included in the same classroom and, in fact, that it is fair to do this so that everyone can be challenged and successful in meeting learning goals.

Collaborative problem solving teaches children to use formal problem-solving strategies such as brainstorming solutions, weighing pros and cons, selecting and implementing the most realistic solution, and monitoring what happens as a result. Children are presented with a "problem" requiring accommodation so that someone can be included and participate fully in the setting or situation. The simple criterion that the children are taught to apply is that the solution has to be fair: that is, an accommodation should neither disadvantage nor advantage someone but represent equality—not sameness.

Table 4 lists the five steps that are part of this collaborative problem-solving process using an example for each step from an elementary grade-level classroom. Take an issue from your own classroom that involves a discrepancy between what is now happening and what you would like to happen, and then work through the steps in terms of how you would approach this problem-solving process. Whenever a teacher initiates a process like this one, it is always a good idea to think about how your students might react to the scenario and how you will both honor their ideas and ensure that proposed solutions are consistent with school and classroom expectations and agreed "rules." You'll want to guide the class discussion so that the children generate strategies that are realistic and then recommend solutions that do reflect agreed values. It is important not to be prescriptive or directive during the brainstorming process in particular, avoiding value judgments while trusting that the children will reach a fair and reasonable conclusion. If restorative practices are ongoing in your school and you as a teacher have engaged your students in taking responsibility for their learning and behavior, the recommended solutions are not only practical but are often directions that adults would not have thought of themselves!

Table 4 An Example of Collaborative Problem Solving in an Elementary Classroom

Collaborative Problem-Solving Steps	The Problem
1. Identify the issue: What is happening that is different from what we would like to happen? (state desired outcomes)	Forgetting writing pens: A few students consistently come to class without the required writing pens or pencils in their backpacks to do their school work. The teacher gives them some to use, but the process repeats itself daily. In addition, students don't ask for a pencil right away (and lose work time) and/or students are disruptive in the way they ask for something to write with.
2. Generate all possible solutions: Brainstorm all solutions without value judgments—encourage creativity.	The class came up with the following ideas: a. Insist that everyone brings a pen to class b. Be sure that students pack their pens in their backpacks at the end of class c. The teacher will keep giving out new pens but will penalize students who keep forgetting d. The teacher will have a set of pens for everyone to use, but collect them at the end of class every day rather than letting students keep them e. The teacher will send a note home to parents telling them how important it is that their child brings a pen to school every day
3. Screen solutions for feasibility: For each possible solution, have the class address two questions: (a) does the solution match our values? and (b) is the solution practical or feasible?	The class agrees that ideas (a), (b), and (d) match our values, but are not sure about (c) and (e) because the punishment doesn't seem to fit the crime. Students also agree that solution (a) probably won't work (as it already isn't working), (e) doesn't seem practical as the teacher would be writing and the parents would be reading lots of notes, and solutions (b) and (d) seem the most feasible though both involve extra transition time and teacher supervision
4. Select a solution to implement: Agree on one or more solutions to implement. Agree that you'll revisit the chosen solution if things don't go well, and the class will try again.	The class agrees to try solution (d): The teacher will have a set number of extra pens that anyone can use (10 is the agreed number for a class of 27 rather than having the full number both to encourage students to continue to bring their own and also to save time getting pens) and that will be collected at the end of the particular lesson or at the end of the day.
5. Evaluate the solution: Talk about whether the solution worked, including discussing	After two weeks, two of the 10 pens seem to have disappeared but 8 are still in the container for anyone to use. The teacher has established a system whereby students check their names on a list if they use a pen that day, and they erase their names when they

Collaborative Problem-Solving Steps	The Problem
each of the following questions: (a) was the issue solved? (b) did the persons involved get what they needed, or are things still not right? (c) how does everyone feel that the collaborative problem-solving process went and what did we learn? and (d) if the solution didn't work or had some other bad results, what should we try next (return to Step 1)?	turn in the pens. One student seems to use a pen from the set every day, but without naming names, the students agree that this is not a big deal as long as he or she puts the pen back every day. The teacher agrees to add two new pens to the set so that there are 10 pens again, and the students agree to try harder to make sure that no pens are missing—checking again every three weeks to see how things are going. The teacher also lets the children know that she isn't going to punish anyone but would like to let parents know—in a positive way—if anyone seems to always be missing something to write with so that they could work together to solve this so that the student doesn't fall behind in work.

BULLYING

Bullying at school creates a multitude of direct and collateral damage; it is also closely related to teen suicide. This section draws on the most recent literature in providing information about effective antibullying models and approaches (as there is more than one). A good example of a complex bullying problem is what happens on school buses where the only adult observer is often the driver who is preoccupied with safe driving. Another complex feature of expectations centered on bullying relates to "cyberbullying" using cell phones, text messages, cell-phone cameras, and web postings of various kinds (Kowalski, Limber, & Agatston, 2008). In high schools, expectations around such behaviors are entirely different than at elementary school: in some cases, low-level bullying is so endemic that the teenage students are not always aware of the acceptable standards of response. Teachers need to develop clear understandings about what bullying is—rather than excuse threatening behavior as "harmless teasing"—and do what they can to encourage students to tell them when bullying is happening so that they can work with the principal to address incidents appropriately.

Identifying Bullying

To address bullying effectively, school personnel and students must acknowledge that some interpersonal interactions may not immediately look like "conflict" but are in fact low-intensity levels of bullying that lead to harm. People often convince themselves that humor generally, and teasing specifically, are innocent behaviors and may even be seen as clever rather than damaging: you may hear someone being urged to "Have a sense of humor" or be told that "We were only teasing." Humor is an important part of human interactions, and one characteristic of good teachers is being able to use humor effectively in teaching and learning interactions (Hindle et al., 2011). But humor that comes at the expense of another person, makes fun of someone, and highlights personal characteristics that can make the other person feel bad is destructive and signals a pattern of bullying. Students and staff must be able to recognize teasing that has gone beyond "good fun," and which can easily be identified through observation of who is laughing—the teaser or the teased? The first step to preventing and addressing bullying is acknowledging bullying as part of a continuum of behavior that is disrespectful, insensitive, and hurtful to others.

Cyberbullying

One of the challenges for supportive schools and classrooms is the need to counter some of the more pernicious aspects of the potential for cyberbullying that has become almost endemic in many schools. The digital age introduces new opportunities for learning but also new risks for harm, sometimes in ways that seem almost invisible, until it is too late to intervene. Cell phones now play a larger role in the life of modern teenagers than television or the Internet, and most teenagers in OECD (Organisation for Economic Co-operation and Development) countries own one. Because one of the prominent features of adolescent personality is impulsivity, electronic tools lend themselves; to acting without much thought—text messages are easy to send; can be an instant response to an assumed insult, personal slight, or rejection; and give the appearance of being victimless in the sense that the recipient of a hostile text is typically not physically in front of the perpetrator. This means that what is called relational aggression is more easily accomplished electronically and girls are more likely to engage in this type of behavior than boys (Coyne, Archer, & Eslea, 2006). Relational aggression, unlike physical aggression, is usually verbal, designed to hurt others' feelings, and causes rejection or conflict within a group. Girls' social groups tend to be relatively stable over time, but factions within the broader group form and re-form frequently as the members try to change their status within the group. Best friends fight, and rifts frequently appear between factions of the groups as the hierarchical relationships shift and re-form (Besag, 2006; Hamilton, 2008).

The activity detailed below can help teachers and students acknowledge and remediate problematic exchanges. As a teacher, you can use this activity format by filling in only one or two examples of common interactions seen at the grade level you teach, then use this format as part of class conferencing and ask the children to fill in other examples and talk about the examples. You can also use the form to invite students to tell you about endemic problems and possible bullying occurring in hallways, the cafeteria, and other common areas: these details can be raised with the principal for further problem solving to prevent and intervene with bullying. Schools need to do more than just identify bullying and tell students not to do it: what are needed are interventions that are age-appropriate and practical for the bully, the victim, and bystanders or observers.

Activity: Discuss the behaviors described below and explain why these are examples of bullying and how you can identify if they are doing harm to others.

The Behavior	When this is bullying:	How can you tell?
Teacher singles out a student who is late to class by saying loudly, "So, you came late to try to avoid the science experiment?"		
Student tells another student on the bus to move to another seat because he prefers that seat.		
A group of students laugh at the answer given by a classmate who didn't understand the teacher's question.		
A teenager receives a series of text messages commenting on her physical appearance.		
A student in first grade is told by two other boys playing a game at recess that he cannot play with them.		

Preventing and Intervening With Bullying

The first step to an antibullying approach in school is for every class-room teacher to assume a proactive approach to preventing bullying. Prevention requires that students have ongoing opportunities to develop strategies for conflict resolution, peer mediation, and responding to threats and dangerous situations in ways that do not escalate the danger but protect and defuse rather than ignore. Conflict Resolution Education (CRE) is an evidence-based approach that teaches students constructive conflict management so that the entire school becomes an environment where teachers and students alike take responsibility for a positive school climate (Garrard & Lipsey, 2007). CRE programs are implemented in the classroom by teachers to facilitate constructive and peaceful resolution of interpersonal conflicts. CRE curricula work to shift win-lose situations to win-win solutions by using conflict in positive ways as opportunities to develop children's skills in empathic listening, anger management, bias awareness, social skills, negotiation, and group problem solving (Daunic, Smith, Robinson, Miller, & Landry, 2000). Regular use of cooperative learning strategies by teachers provides a positive context for increasing students' interpersonal skills and understandings. These approaches should begin at school entry so that by the time students reach middle school—when peer conflict is particularly salient as well as hurtful—they are equipped with the social skills to prevent bullying and avoid engaging in incidents that evolve into bullying.

Specific bullying intervention programs typically focus on the bully or the victim, or both. They mesh well with CRE approaches but bullying interventions are better suited to adult mediation rather than peer mediation given that bullying is characterized by peer conflict and peer power relationships. The first step in any antibullying program is to have agreed processes in place for children to report bullying incidents to a trusted adult—a teacher, counselor, or other staff member at school—without risk to their psychological or physical safety. This requires some discussion among staff, as bullying doesn't generally occur in the presence of teachers but in places where adult supervision is less evident, such as on the playground or school bus, or in the cafeteria or hallways. Teachers must also acknowledge that bullying takes various forms: physical violence may be easier to recognize, but malicious gossip or texts and social exclusion from play groups at recess are also forms of bullying that cause harm.

The Olweus Bullying Prevention Program is well known and has undergone over two decades of research on its effectiveness and adaptability to different educational contexts (Bauer, Lozano, & Rivara, 2007; Olweus, 2003). The approach builds on a set of key principles for the school environment that are consistent with the Restorative School

Discipline approach: (1) adults must show warmth towards and interest in students; (2) there are consistent expectations for prosocial behavior; (3) violations of expectations are met with restorative not punitive consequences; and (4) adults in the school act as role models for nonbullying interactions with one another and with children.

RESTORATIVE CLASSROOM DISCIPLINE STRUCTURES AND PROCESSES

Restorative school discipline begins fundamentally in the classroom. We have discussed how classroom climate reflects the teaching and learning relationships of the teacher with children and that of children with one another, facilitated by an emotionally intelligent teacher who recognizes that students cannot learn effectively in an environment where they are disrespected and socially excluded (Evans & Harvey, 2012). Restorative practices are all about restoring good relationships and making amends following conflict that has caused harm. Thus, the first step has to be ensuring that the ethos of the school and every classroom supports the peaceful resolution of conflict—which is perhaps inevitable in any human environment—and enables children to make restitution without losing dignity and respect.

Zehr (1990, 2002) highlights that any interpersonal conflict between a victim and an offender must be addressed by focusing where the problem begins—within the relationship. As emphasized throughout the guide, the major purposes of restorative practices are not to blame and punish but to heal damaged relationships while preserving the personal dignity of those involved. Restorative practices had their origins in the criminal justice system—under the framework of *restorative justice*—but have been widely adapted for use in schools by educators and families, with rigorous evaluations of effectiveness carried out in Australia, New Zealand, England, and Scotland.

This section of the teacher's guide provides details, implementation of restorative curricula, mediation, and restorative meeting and conferencing that are essential for restorative practices in the classroom.

Restorative Curricula

Restorative curricula are based on several key principles underpinning a restorative justice approach to peace and conflict resolution:

- *Interpersonal relationships:* Affirming positive interpersonal relationships in the school community without exclusion and deficit theorizing that places blame on individual children, families, or other persons

- *Personal dignity:* Preserving the personal dignity of all members of the school community, encompassing the idea that every person belongs, is valued and cared for, and has the right to be treated fairly
- *Mutual respect and understanding:* Sharing each person's perspective about what happened in conflict, accompanied by respect for different views as constructed realities with strong personal meaning for each participant
- *Restorative conferencing:* Commitment to conflict resolution and restoration of positive interpersonal relationships through conversation in a safe environment
- *Restitution:* Agreement regarding what needs to happen to set things right, defuse conflict, and restore positive relationships

Cavanaugh (2007) provides helpful advice for schools about the developmental implementation of a restorative practices approach to conflict resolution. He also describes how these approaches can build children's social-emotional capacities and help to prevent bullying. For this to happen, teachers and all other school personnel must reflect reasonable expectations for young people based on social-emotional abilities developing at different ages:

- *Ages 5 to 6:* Children can understand feelings by learning that everyone has feelings and that different people can have different feelings—that is, feelings may not be the same. Children start to develop empathy by "bonding" with one another in ways that allow them to see how the other child feels about something. This is the time when children begin to learn about what a friendship is, compared with simply playing with one another.
- *Ages 7 to 9:* Children now understand the dynamics of friendships and belonging to a group. They learn about listening, trusting, speaking honestly "from the heart," and they learn to be respectful of others. This is the age when children should begin to learn negotiation and mediation skills rather than simply pushing one's own perspectives or desires at the expense of others.
- *Ages 10 to 11:* In addition to all the above skills and understandings, children can speak truthfully while showing respect—they can be diplomatic. They should develop peacemaking skills and know how to solve problems in groups (e.g., through conferencing).
- *Ages 12 to 14:* Teenagers can engage in restorative conversations that do not confuse the problem with the person. They can take on major

responsibility to conduct problem-solving group conferences, either formally in classrooms or informally with a peer group and with friends.

- *Ages 15 to 17:* Teenagers can facilitate communication between bullies and victims, restore dignity to both parties, and negotiate removal of blame and punishment.

It is important for school personnel to reflect reasonable expectations that children can develop prosocial skills and understanding as they progress through the grades. Some expectations are not age-appropriate: for example, adults should not expect six-year-olds to be diplomatic in talking about one's own feelings, but children at this age can be expected to listen to how the other person feels and be able to describe them as evidence of having listened. Nor do skills that may be developmentally reasonable develop simply through maturation. Most teenagers will not be good at engaging in "restorative conversations that do not confuse the problem with the person"—indeed most adults have difficulty with this! Teenagers are ready to learn how to do this, but these skills will be the product of previous social skill development as well as current expectations and supports for doing so.

In the classroom, the teacher can plan systematically to teach restorative principles while being careful to build on children's capacities at different stages of development. The best approach is to design a series of lessons or activities for all students rather than being focused solely on children who have challenging behavior or being reactive in response to incidents. In these whole-class activities, ask students to consider challenging issues: you might, for example, ask students to discuss a recent local incident involving charges of racism that was featured in the local newspaper or they could discuss a media report of text bullying. The focus of these discussions is to practice using *restorative language and scripts* that illuminate the importance of understanding events and their impact on the people involved.

A Generic Restorative Script:

- What happened?
- What do you think about what happened?
- What might someone else think about what happened?
- Who has been affected by what happened?
- In what way?
- What do you think has to happen next to make things better?

As you become more experienced in using the script, you'll develop the flexibility needed to vary the questions to fit particular events and circumstances. You will also be able to adapt this basic script to fit children's language and culture.

In addition to using a semiformal script like this in group discussions with students, teachers can engage in and thus model active nonjudgmental listening skills with the intent of developing those skills in children as well. We often leap to interpretations that fit our preconceived ideas about people and events, failing to hear people out and failing to listen to information that would give us a far clearer and more accurate picture of what happened. In addition, listening carefully to someone—whether that person is another professional or a child—communicates fundamental respect to the person, just as failing to hear the "other side of the story" shuts people down and communicates a kind of righteous assertion of a power imbalance. The following examples illustrate restorative language that you can use to initiate discussion of an incident or challenge:

- *Can someone tell me what happened?*
- *Can I tell you what happened from my perspective? Does anyone else see it differently?*
- *How do you feel about that?*
- *Could you each tell me how you see things? Let's have XXXX go first and after she has finished, XXXX can give his perspective. After both of you have explained what happened, then we can try to sort this out.*

In these kinds of conversations, the teacher takes a neutral perspective and tries to support students to identify on their own what needs to be done to either put things right or move on if the problem cannot be solved just then. School personnel should be prepared to use this nonconfrontational conversation anywhere, for example, if there has been a negative interaction between students in the school lunchroom.

Mediation

The restorative script and the development of understandings for restorative practices described above illustrate informal mediation and teaching opportunities that the teacher can use: individuals or groups are being asked to consider the cause of an incident and also different perspectives on that incident with a view towards reaching consensus on how to move forward. However, these informal conversations may not be sufficient for conflict in many situations, particularly when it is obvious that different participants in a conflict situation are miles apart in their perceptions of the incident and what needs to happen next. Where conflict has caused harm or whenever both parties feel strongly that the other person is the cause of the problem, formal mediation will be needed. Mediation is a process in which those involved in conflict are supported by a neutral third party—the mediator—who serves as a facilitator to enable everyone to hear different perspectives and to find a mutually acceptable way forward (Kane et al., 2007). Mediation differs from the more typical process of having a designated person in authority that metes out justice when an offender is sent to the office by a teacher or other school staff member. In mediation, those who are involved in the conflict are viewed as being in the best position to identify ways to resolve that conflict, make amends for any harm caused, and decide how to move forward. Thus, the offender and the "offended" are part of the mediation process. Evaluation is equally important. Whenever a mediation system is in place, there should be a procedure for logging incidents so that the school can evaluate whether the mediation initiative is having a positive impact, no effect, or might even be associated with an increase in incidents.

Peer mediation

In schools, the mediator is likely to be a teacher or someone who provides support services such as a school counselor or a deputy principal. However, students at middle and high school levels can also be trained to carry out peer mediation, particularly where there is a strong school culture of informal conferencing and restorative scripts operating in classrooms across the school years. Peer mediation could be expected on the playground, for example, at recess and lunchtime with some less formal support from school personnel assigned as supervisors at that time. Peer mediators could be older peers who volunteer to mediate conflict on the playground involving younger students under the watchful eye of the adult supervisor. Organizing a peer mediation system for nonclassroom settings can be a productive activity for a school's home/school partnership program that can organize and run buddy restorative workshops for all students (Kane et al., 2007). Ongoing records that are kept for playground accidents, postrecess referrals, and "on-the-fence" discipline-type consequences for conflict can be examined to determine whether incidents such as these are decreasing in frequency and intensity or both. These records can be examined periodically to evaluate whether informal mediation networks are working effectively in reducing challenging behavior incidents on the playground.

The selection of peer mediators is important. Teachers have an important role in identifying potential peer mediators by inviting student applications and nominations, or through teacher nominations. One problem with these processes is that they often result in identifying students as mediators who are considered to be exemplary and who are school leaders (Algozzine, Daunic, & Smith, 2010). This presents an issue of credibility and relevance for the students who are referred as offenders. Undoubtedly, student leaders are selected because as top students they exhibit "teacher-like" characteristics such as being responsible and self-managing. As student leaders, however, top students may be quite unlike the students referred for mediation who may be disengaged and even hostile to the school. For mediation to work, it must be socially acceptable to all participants—including the student who is referred for problem behavior (Robinson, Smith, & Daunic, 2000). Blake, Wang, Cartledge, and Gardner (2000) demonstrated that students who had a history of behavioral problems can be trained to be effective trainers in teaching social skills to others. Algozinne (2010) and colleagues suggest that peer mediators who themselves have shown high levels of interpersonal conflict at school "have the potential to become peer mediators and, in so doing, enhance a program's overall acceptability" (p. 120). In addition, cultural factors should be considered in identifying particular peer mediators for a given situation: whenever possible, peer mediators should share cultural understandings with the offender and any student victims.

Shuttle mediation

Shuttle mediation is a term describing situations where at least one of the parties involved in a conflict is afraid, unwilling, or unable to meet face-to-face with others who are involved. In shuttle mediation, the mediator moves back and forth between those involved in the conflict. The mediator might first listen to the student's side of the story, then hear what the teacher has to say, then go back to the student to discuss what the teacher said, then go back to the teacher to discuss what the student said, and so on.

Mentoring

Mentoring is another widely used approach for supporting students who are judged at risk for or who already exhibit behavioral and educational difficulties. The establishment of mentoring programs is generally a school decision supported by the school board, which is made by the principal in consultation with other personnel, including teachers. An informal type of mentoring is available within classrooms as follow-up to the peer support networks established by teachers in their classrooms. More formal mentoring programs involve students across the school working with other students at different grade levels (e.g., a peer tutoring program where students in fourth grade might mentor new readers in Grades 1–2) and with persons from outside the school who serve as mentors (e.g., college students who might mentor high school seniors planning for their transition to university study) or both. Peer mentoring programs are not an effective strategy to work with younger children who have ongoing behavioral challenges: while the role of peers and classmates may be part of intervention planning, the focus is on preparing children for positive interactions with one another—not to prepare one child to remediate another. Mentoring programs are not particularly effective in dealing with young people who have already engaged in serious antisocial and illegal acts. Mentoring can be extremely valuable as a prevention program, particularly for young people who have limited access to effective adult role models, and mentors may also be extremely helpful as potential mediators as part of carefully structured interventions.

Information to support the establishment of mentoring programs in schools is included in the School Leader's Guide. That guide incorporates basic information on what mentoring is, what the research literature tells us about what can and cannot be achieved through mentoring, and a description of mentoring programs that have been shown to be effective.

RESTORATIVE CLASSROOM CONFERENCING

The previous sections describe the groundwork laid by the school and the teacher for Restorative Classroom Discipline, including attention to behavior expectations, classroom climate, ongoing peer supports for positive social relationships and interpersonal interactions, collaborative problem solving to address issues and conflict, and individualized approaches to mediation and mentoring. Even with these in place, there are occasions when a formal restorative classroom conference is needed for more serious challenges that have the potential to cause harm to individual children. In such instances, the situation may have already escalated to the point that a school restorative conference is required. However, there will be instances where the first step is for the teacher to undertake an in-class restorative conference to prevent serious conflict from erupting or before disagreements escalate into conflict.

Teachers can use "circles" or circle time regularly in their classrooms, and their use is particularly common with young students as the way to start and finish the day. This use of circles in the lower elementary grades is useful in establishing that the first thing that happens is getting together with the teacher to find out what happens next. As the children are familiar with a practice such as sitting on the floor in a circle on the rug, they can easily be asked to gather together in a circle at other times if the teacher wants to discuss an important issue that has arisen. However, circle time, as generally used by teachers in elementary school, is not the same as conferencing to address a challenge or discipline problem.

In-class restorative conferencing shares some features with a "circle" activity but needs to be age-appropriate and follow formal guidelines that are well understood by the students. Calling a restorative classroom conference might be the teacher's response to reports of name-calling at recess by children in the class (elementary school) or an antagonistic *ad hominem* (character attack) discussion that happened in a lesson the previous day when it was too late in the class period to address (secondary school). Teachers who call in-class restorative conferences should follow the general script for restorative conversations but with variations for issues and incidents depending on whether individuals or groups are the target of harm:

- Describing the incident or events that have led to the conference (e.g., "Yesterday while students were working in their groups on your project related to immigration, I heard several negative statements about particular immigrant groups—suggesting they were somehow not desirable or wanted. I think it would be helpful to discuss this important issue.")
- Placing the problem in context and exploring alternative interpretations (e.g., "Historically, different groups have been discriminated against in the United States. Not many years ago, people criticized immigrants from Italy and Ireland, now what groups are criticized? Why do you think this is the case?")
- Reaching consensus about possible negative effects if the problem isn't resolved (e.g., "Given international relationships and persons whom we know who are living in our region who came here from Country X, why is this issue important?")
- Reconciliation (e.g., "How can we ensure that someone we know isn't harmed by these attitudes?")
- Restoration (e.g., "What kinds of things would promote more positive attitudes toward and harmony among different people?")

Teachers can also use less formal approaches such as having restorative "chats" or miniconferences with two or more students (Varnham, 2008) or asking students to engage in "restorative thinking" about an issue.

SUMMARY

This chapter covers strategies for teacher use in regular classrooms to establish peer networks and other supports to ensure that the principles of restorative classroom practices are translated into reality. Approaches such as cooperative learning and interventions for bullying are well researched, and regular education initiatives like these are expected to be in place to support student learning and behavior prior to referrals for individualized services. Indeed, in most U.S. states, as authorized by the Individuals with Disabilities Education Improvement Act (IDEIA), schools are required to show evidence that these kinds of strategies are implemented first, before eligibility for special education is assessed. The chapter also deals with general principles and practices for Restorative Classroom Discipline, including mediation, mentoring, and classroom conferencing. To address situations where the types of interventions described in this chapter haven't worked, we next cover the foundations for planning individualized interventions (Chapter 6) and provide a range of exemplars to illustrate the essential four components for effective interventions (Chapter 7).

6 Interventions for Individual Students

Child-Focused Planning

Schoolwide behavior expectations and the principles of restorative practices described in the earlier chapters of this guide address the kinds of behavior challenges typical, at various times, of many individual children and of students in the general school population. This chapter and Chapter 7 focus on interventions for students whose behavioral challenges are more severe and persistent or both, thus requiring structured and individualized planning to enable them to learn and to ensure their own and others' safety. As we explained, school climate factors, such as a restorative ethos, positive and accepting attitudes, and warm emotional classroom atmospheres, are still highly relevant, prerequisite requirements.

Classroom teachers, however, will almost certainly need access to specialist advice to help them implement secondary interventions for as many as 15 percent of their students who present social, emotional, and behavioral challenges at some time during the school year. Another 2 to 5 percent of the school population exhibit ongoing and more severe behavioral difficulties that require specialist consultation to design tertiary intervention programs that may also entail supplemental services outside school. The necessary background requirements for such specialized and individualized intervention plans are explained in this chapter; the next chapter describes and illustrates specific intervention strategies with more detailed examples. First, we need to consider what is meant by these different levels of behavioral concern.

SECONDARY AND TERTIARY PREVENTION AND INTERVENTION

In 1996, Walker and his colleagues published their description of the three-level approach to organizing intervention supports and services for students with emotional and behavioral disorders. This approach has now been widely adopted across the United States. According to this model, specific prevention or intervention approaches are tailored to the three levels—primary (Level 1), secondary (Level 2), and tertiary (Level 3). The original cascade model of services for special education utilized a pyramid to illustrate roughly the different percentages of children who would need different levels of support and services, starting from the broad base of regular education to the point of the pyramid with services for those requiring the most intensive support.

According to the three-level approach, primary or Level 1 supports parallel the broad base in referring to the majority of children in school who respond positively to what Walker et al. (1996) termed "universal interventions," comprising schoolwide discipline guidelines, instruction in selected interpersonal skills such as conflict resolution, and effective teaching and schooling. Most children are eager to learn. They typically pay attention, listen to teacher instructions, interact positively with classmates, engage in learning activities, and do their best on classroom assignments, homework, and assessments. These children generally do not require ongoing services other than occasional reminders, since they can at times make mistakes, get frustrated, overreact, bring problems from home to school, and sometimes get into or cause trouble for teachers and peers. Generally, however, their difficulties are short-lived and respond well to evidence-based regular education practices (including small group interventions that can be conducted within regular education classes).

Fuchs, Fuchs, and Stecker (2010) note that the Individuals with Disabilities Education Improvement Act (IDEIA) as a special education entitlement builds on the expectation that schools already have in place empirically based Level 1 schoolwide programs. Appropriate use of special education services relies on a solid foundation of regular education with ongoing activities to ensure that grade-level curricula and pedagogies are research-based practices that have been shown to be effective in promoting positive learning and behavior for the majority of children (Cheney, Flower, & Templeton, 2008). Among these are evidence-based pedagogical practices such as cooperative learning, direct instruction, and peer tutoring. Similarly, we describe strategies and systems for schoolwide discipline (see especially Chapters 1, 2, and 4) that also represent Level 1 approaches demonstrated to be effective for managing the behavior of the majority of students who only rarely break school rules. The percentage of students whose needs are met by these primary Level 1 approaches is generally accepted to be approximately 80 to 85 percent (Curwin & Mendler, 1999; Wanzek & Vaughn, 2009).

Secondary and tertiary level services are for those students whose needs go beyond regular education services (Gresham, 2005). Secondary prevention, or Level 2, refers to the approximately 15 percent of children in school who will periodically require additional specialized services and support, such as small group or embedded tutoring services. This percentage of the school population includes high incidence diagnoses such as learning disabilities and mild-moderate behavioral disorders. Burns and Gibbons (2008) describe what is now called the response-to-intervention (RTI) model and explain how making special education services available early, rather than waiting for students to fail, enhances services to children. Level 2 services may involve individualized in-class tutoring, resource room instruction, and in some cases part- to full-time placements in self-contained classrooms. Much of the discussion and debate around the effectiveness of the response-to-intervention policy involves the extent to which an early response to identified educational needs can preclude placement in more stigmatizing programs requiring diagnostic labels. There is an expectation that Level 2 services are not permanent for individual children but represent additional support required for different time periods and across school years—though IDEIA requires periodic evaluation to make these decisions.

Finally, some children and youth in school, such as the real-life individuals we describe later in this chapter and the following one, exhibit learning and behavioral needs requiring intensive tertiary Level 3 support for extended periods of time (perhaps all through the school years), which is designed to prevent more serious escalation of the students' difficulties. Children requiring Level 3 interventions may exhibit persistent, severe, and evolving behavioral challenges and have been diagnosed as having a conduct disorder, developmental disability, and/or emotional disorder; these children require longer-term individualized interventions. They may have dual diagnoses such as autism and intellectual disability, or oppositional defiant disorder and severe learning disability. Fuchs et al. (2010) report that up to 5 percent of school-age students in the United States prove to be unresponsive to secondary or Level 2 interventions, requiring this more intensive intervention at Level 3.

Regular education was originally intended for the majority of children who respond well to primary prevention approaches. As a system, regular education has done less well with children who require secondary prevention supports and has typically excluded those who require tertiary Level 3 interventions. Historically, special education was designed primarily to address secondary and tertiary support needs, but it also has performed below expectations with students exhibiting severe behavioral challenges. These two chapters deal with all children who evidence difficulty following the school's behavioral expectations, ranging from those only occasionally requiring support to those whose problem behaviors are severe and ongoing. Both this chapter and Chapter 7 focus on behaviors that are disruptive, stressful, and raise safety concerns for classmates, the teacher, and the students themselves.

One approach that schools have used to reduce seriously challenging behavior has been the adoption of "zero-tolerance" policies designed to respond immediately and intensely to violent and disruptive behavior in schools. This policy has not worked well, and a review of 10 years of research reports reveals that zero-tolerance practices have actually been associated with *increases* in challenging behavior and school dropout rates (American Psychological Association Zero Tolerance Task Force, 2006). Greene (2008) explains that zero-tolerance punitive responses to behaviors are not effective with children who have social, emotional, and behavior challenges because they typically do not have the skills to behave differently. In contrast, our three present guides integrate evidence-based schoolwide and classroomwide systemic approaches with individualized interventions that span all levels of need.

IMPLICATIONS: APPLYING GENERAL PRINCIPLES

If we are going to be able to design interventions for those students who require Level 2 and 3 intensities of support yet fit within the general ethos of a comprehensive restorative discipline approach, certain fundamental realities need to be considered and addressed. The first is that if we are talking about 15 percent of all students (and maybe only 2–5 percent in some more extreme cases) exhibiting problematic behavior, we cannot underestimate the seriousness of some of the challenges facing schools. We have to be realistic about the difficulties presented by some students to educational institutions set up on the assumption that young people know how to behave, voluntarily follow rules, have social-emotional competencies, and are motivated to learn and to succeed. Nevertheless, it is important not to catastrophize about these difficulties. Focusing on the negatives, emphasizing deficits, and abandoning positive efforts before they have been adequately tested may relieve the immediate problem for a school, by means of exclusion, but has negative repercussions for society in the longer term. An evidence-driven, strengths-based, comprehensive approach is not some Pollyanna fantasy but an eminently practical method when properly implemented. In the following sections, we first look at the general principles needed to make interventions workable for teachers. The general principles are (a) avoiding deficit theorizing, (b) recognizing barriers to change, (c) always thinking about culture, (d) working as a team (which includes the student and his or her family), and (e) in all intervention planning, relying on the powerful social influences of the individuals who really shape a young person's world. These people are referred to as mediators, and we will discuss ways of engaging them in the process of change.

A High School Example: Jayla

We begin this part of the discussion with a practical example of a high school student known to us. Jayla is 15 years old; her mother is African American and her father (whom she has never met) is white. She lives with her mother, an adult half-brother who works a night shift as a security guard, and her half-sister, who has three young children. Her half-sister is unemployed and receiving welfare benefits. Jayla's mother, however, has a responsible job as a medical receptionist and the family enjoys a moderate, lower middle-class lifestyle. Jayla's progress through elementary school was unremarkable despite the fact that her mother moved a lot and Jayla had six changes of school prior to her current high school, where she is in 10th grade. Jayla has not done well this year. She says her schoolwork is "boring" and she is getting a reputation for being disruptive in class. She joined a group of girls she wants to impress but is not well accepted by them. She started smoking dope (marijuana), and some teachers attribute her increasingly bizarre behavior to getting high before coming to school. This semester she started swearing at teachers, being confrontational and aggressive (bullying others), resulting in two episodes of suspension. Matters came to a head a few weeks ago when it was ascertained that she set fire to the school's assembly hall, and previously, although undetected at the time, lit a fire in the female bathrooms. The school was initiating an expulsion process. What do you immediately think about Jayla's situation? What would you recommend? Before jumping into details, consider the following four background conditions.

AVOIDING DEFICIT DISCUSSIONS ABOUT CHILDREN

Teachers have a major impact on how the school community thinks about students who exhibit challenging behavior. Rather than emphasizing student deficits and shortcomings, teachers need to adopt a strengths-based approach to planning and problem solving. All students have some support needs and are in the process of acquiring the multitude of understandings, competencies, and skills to become productive, prosocial adults who make valued contributions to their communities. Like others, children who display chronic behavior difficulties have certain strengths, even when these are increasingly overshadowed by negative factors as the year progresses and they gain a "reputation" in the school. Children may start the school year with their bad behavior from the previous year following them relentlessly, so they don't really have a chance to start fresh with a new teacher who isn't immediately on guard—waiting for the student to put a foot wrong. When a student has a reputation for being a problem at school, this also places teachers at risk for blaming those problems on *deficits within the child*. It becomes tempting to engage in deficit thinking that lures teachers and others into minimizing agency—their potential for making a difference in the life of that child.

Greene (2008) has written a powerful book about children who are *lost at school*. He urges all of us to take a long hard look at conversations about children which actually reveal the underlying negative attitudes and interpretations going far beyond behavioral evidence. Table 5 can be used to stimulate discussion about the kinds of negative comments that undermine restorative approaches with individual children. Teachers are in an excellent position to brainstorm with one another respectful but constructively critical responses to different examples of deficit thinking that might arise in conversation and in formal discussion about individual students.

Table 5 Re-Thinking Negative Conversations About Children With Challenging Behavior

Comment	Questions	Possible Responses
He does that to get attention.	But isn't it okay for a child to want attention? Is he getting attention when he is doing something positive? Does the child know what to do to get attention in positive ways?	- teach positive attention
She wants things her way.	Don't we all want things our way at least some of the time? Does the child know how to negotiate getting what she wants some of the time?	- let them make decisions; guide them
He's being manipulative.	Does this child really have the skills to be manipulative, intentionally? -yes If he is pushing my buttons, is this really his fault or is it because I'm not controlling my behavior as the adult?	- follow through; be firm

Comment	Questions	Possible Responses
She just doesn't care about learning/ school.	Would she have any good reason to care—is school a positive place for her? Is she having any success at all in learning, or is school mostly punishing for him?	*-positive environment make her enjoy school*
He makes bad choices.	Is it possible that the "bad choice" he makes ends up getting him what he wants? Would an alternative "good choice" lead to a positive outcome for him? Does he have the skills to make other choices?	*-make sure he knows good & bad consequences*
She comes from a bad home.	Why is this relevant to her relationships and behavior in school? *- irrelevant* What do we really know about her home anyway? And even if the home is dysfunctional, why can't school be a positive experience for her?	*-classroom can still be positive*
He's naughty.	Maybe, but when our own children are naughty, don't we intervene? What are we doing to make "being naughty" functional for him? Is he naughty all the time, or only in certain circumstances, certain places, and with certain people? Why?	*-find out why; positive & negative reinforcement + punishment*
She behaves that way because she's mentally ill, because she has ADHD, etc.	Does repeating the child's disability "label" really explain this particular incident? *-no* How can we build on her strengths rather than emphasize "what's wrong"? *-don't single her out*	*-focus on what she does well, accomodate for her.*
His older brother was exactly the same/just as bad.	Is it possible that the whole family is stigmatized at this school—so this child doesn't have a chance to do well? Is the older brother's behavior relevant to what to do with this child? If we weren't successful in turning around the older brother, can we do a better job with this child? *- yes*	*-don't judge, or listen to reputation -get to know the students*

Source: Based on a discussion in Greene (2008), pp. 12–13.

Quickly, think back to how you might have reacted to Jayla. Did you ask yourself about her academic potential? Actually it is quite high: her score on the Wechsler Intelligence Scale for Children was above average and her reading is at an 11th-grade level. Did you think about what her career ambitions might be or whether she knows anything about what it is like to go to college? Did you ask yourself if she has any sporting skills? Actually she used to be quite an accomplished tennis player and the Williams sisters, Venus and Serena, are her idols. Does she play a musical instrument? Her mother's boyfriend encouraged her interest in playing the guitar.

UNDERSTANDING BARRIERS TO CHANGE

In his recent book, *Outliers: The Story of Success*, Malcolm Gladwell (2008) shows very convincingly that it is a myth that highly successful people achieved great heights purely on the basis of their own innate brilliance. Successful sports stars, musicians, business people, entrepreneurs, all had unique opportunities and supports—yes, they had ability, talent, and drive but they also had historical opportunities, worked hard, practiced long hours, and were in the right place at the right time. We can apply roughly the same analysis to conceptualizing children who are the opposite of a success. What external factors and past circumstances have contributed to their apparent failure, and how can we mitigate these barriers to positive change? The most common major barriers to change that we need to consider when designing interventions include family dysfunction, negative peer influences, missing out on developmental stages resulting in a lack of general skills such as problem solving or actively coping with emotion, absence of a clear cultural and personal identity, and financial stresses such as unemployment and inadequate housing.

Jayla does not represent some tragic, hard-luck story (although some of your students will indeed have such stories). She was never sexually abused, does not live in poverty or a crime-ridden neighborhood, has never gone hungry, or had a life-threatening illness. But her father left her mother before she was born and her mother had two children from different men before that. Her mother has a good job but works very long hours; her level of supervision of Jayla has never been very high. The three young children in the household get a lot of attention and Jayla is often pressured into providing child care for her little nieces and nephew. Changing schools frequently made it harder for her to develop steady friendship patterns or have a close girlfriend; as a result she lacks self-confidence and assertiveness skills to resist peer pressure. Her current high school is predominantly white and Jayla struggles with her identity as a light-skinned African American. She is less sexually experienced than many of the girls in her class.

RESTORATIVE PRACTICES THAT ARE CULTURALLY RESPONSIVE

As we already stressed the importance of cultural issues (Chapter 5), we illustrate this background principle of intervention planning by describing another student we know.

An Elementary School Example: Nikotemo

Nikotemo is an 8-year-old boy whose family comes from Samoa, although he himself was born in California. He lives with his mother Aveolela and younger brother Apelu. Nikotemo is a good looking boy with a cheeky grin and a love of anything to do with playing outside—he's a good swimmer and a very fast runner. His classroom behavior is causing his elementary teacher a lot of headaches. He resists all academic work, and if directed firmly to comply, he flicks books on the floor, tips pencils out of containers, lashes out at other students, and recently threw a drink bottle around the class, hitting another child. He seems to show no empathy for the children he upsets or hurts.

But his teacher Gayle is most concerned and anxious about his recent use of inappropriate sexual comments and actions. On two occasions, Nikotemo has simulated masturbation in front of other younger children (this is a mixed second- and third-grade class in a Catholic school). He recently defecated on the toilet floor during a lunch break and exposed himself to a group of students on another occasion. Other parents have expressed concern to the principal and told their children not to play with or have anything to do with Nikotemo.

In the next chapter, we describe what some aspects of the program for Nikotemo's so-called sexualized behavior were like, but for now we want to explain that his teacher, despite being very upset by his conduct, was determined to try to understand this boy to the best of her ability. Gayle invited Aveolela to come to the school to talk privately with her. Before doing so, she contacted the pastor of a Samoan Catholic church in town, and without revealing any confidential family details asked him for some advice. He provided her with many insights: He told her that the family's Samoan last name, Igoa, is pronounced "ingoa," that it was important to check that the mother wasn't working at the time of the appointment, that she should be invited to bring a friend or older family member along to the meeting, and that coffee and fruit juice and maybe some snacks should be served at the meeting. He also instructed that Gayle should spend quite some time getting acquainted with the family, even giving a little of her own background, before launching into a discussion of Nikotemo's problems.

Gayle thanked him for this cultural advice but said she really wanted to know what their lifestyle, beliefs, and values might be like. The pastor smiled and said he couldn't possibly generalize about such matters and that her best strategy was to ask Aveolela directly. This she did, but found it hard going. Aveolela saw Nikotemo's behavior as a direct consequence of her having had the child out of wedlock—it was God's punishment. But as for Samoan ways, she was doing all she could to put island life behind her and be a proper American. She did not like to mix with other Samoan immigrants and she did not speak Samoan at home with the two boys. However, she acknowledged that her mother April (Nikotemo's grandmother), who lived at the house, helped out with child care and did not speak very good English.

Gayle did exactly what she should have done. Because she found out something about Samoan social expectations, her meeting with Aveolela was very successful. They clicked right away and this mother said she was eager to help in any way she could. Because Gayle was willing to ask about lifestyle and beliefs and values and seemed genuinely interested and respectful, she learned about the family's religious affiliations, basic dynamics, and what they were striving to accomplish. She learned what Aveolela was worried about and what she wanted Nikotemo to achieve. Before going to the professional meeting called to discuss Nikotemo's case, Gayle jotted down some notes for herself (see below).

- Mom is trying to establish a solely "white"/mainstream American identity—not really working
- N is possibly confused regarding his own ethnic and cultural identity
- Grandma is an unknown factor—can she handle the child care with no English?
- Mom has never heard of ADHD—"God's punishment" is her hypothesis. Blames herself?
- Lack of contact with Samoan or Pacific Island community in Long Beach leaves mom socially isolated?
- Mom's English isn't great; grandma has none—are N's verbal skills less than we realize?

From the limited information provided about this situation, would you add anything to this list? The key point is that unless we consider the cultural background of the student and his or her family, we are not treating the family as equal partners in finding solutions and we cannot anticipate causal influences that represent barriers to change. As a result, we are unlikely to plan interventions that "fit" the realities of children's lives.

INCORPORATING MEDIATOR PERSPECTIVES AND CAPABILITIES

It should be apparent that anyone with any degree of involvement in the student's situation needs to work together with everyone else in the team. This theme occurs again and again throughout this guide, but is addressed in more detail in Chapter 8. But many of the really important influences in a student's life are not professional educators, counselors, or mental health experts. They are the ordinary people with whom the student spends most of his or her time, so this becomes a vital background dimension to the design of interventions. All behavioral programs are put in place—whether directly (and planfully) or indirectly (naturalistically)—by persons who have a relationship with and some degree of influence on the young person of concern. These "significant others" are *mediators* in that they have a mediating effect on the student—now and in the future—and how they carry out this mediating role can in turn make the difference between a successful or unsuccessful intervention program.

The past literature on intervening with behavior challenges tended to emphasize formal training for mediators to ensure that they have the skills and understandings needed to be effective as intervention agents. While these skills are important, an exclusive focus on skill building runs the risk of neglecting the need to attend to the relationship between the child and the adult mediator. By the time a student is referred for formal intervention of some kind, it is likely the student's relationships with others have also been affected—sometimes quite negatively. It may even be that a teacher actually has grown to dislike the student, and rather than experience negative feelings she may avoid interactions altogether with that student. But as we have already indicated, the child needs to feel cared for and valued in order to be motivated to change to new behaviors that those adults expect: Children know when they are not liked, even when adults have convinced themselves and others that they are showing no visible signs of rejection. Thus, we advocate a procedure called *positive affective priming* (Evans, 2010) as a useful step in the intervention process, enabling the adult who interacts with the child to experience positive feelings that then have a positive impact on future interactions.

Activity: Positive Affective Priming

Rationale: In cases where there has been conflict between the teacher and a student for whom a formal behavior intervention program is developed, the teacher may harbor negative attitudes towards that child. Unless acknowledged and addressed, these negative

(Continued)

(Continued)

attitudes may later interfere with establishing the kinds of positive interpersonal interactions needed for the child's efforts to be rewarded by the teacher. The teacher needs to view the student in a different, more positive light.

What to Do: The teacher might ask the student's mother or father if they would share some photographs of the student starting at a very young age to the present. These photographs should be ones that the family and the student like a great deal, including photographs of the student smiling, playing a game that he or she enjoys, being positive, being nice to a younger sibling, and so on. If the parents are reluctant to loan the photos to the teacher to take home for 2 to 3 days, ask the parents if they would meet with you after school and look at the photos with you: This could actually be a very pleasant experience for the teacher and the family. If there is such a meeting with the family, remember that the purpose of the photo viewing is to see another side of the child, so this is not the time to talk about problems or revisit conflict. Keep the focus of the time together on positive stories about the pictures!

Follow-Up: After the teacher has viewed the photos, reflect on the student's good points and how nice he or she looked in so many of the pictures you saw. Think of new information and things you know about the student that you didn't know before. Does he or she have a pet you can ask about? What does he or she like to do with the family on weekends? Can you think of what nice things you might say to him or her even before class starts to set a positive tone for your relationship with this student?

As the child's teacher, you are one of the child's most significant mediators and you interact with other mediators who interact with that same child every day, including the child's peers. Understanding the influences of mediators—teachers, friends, family—is important. Parents, for example, are crucial mediators in the life of a child and how they react to the child's challenging behavior and improved behavior is critical. If we expect too much of parents in relationship to a teenage "child," do we undermine and complicate further that parent's ability to support positive behavior change? And how might the teacher-student relationship be negatively affected if we fail to acknowledge what the teacher expects and needs as well as what the student expects and needs? Finally, friends can mediate whether or not an intervention is successful or fails—and the absence of even one positive (mediator) friend for support can make it doubly challenging to motivate a teenager to be part of the school community. Completing the *Mediator Worksheet* as a team helps develop appreciation of mediator perspectives on behavioral challenges relevant to intervention (see Figure 4).

Figure 4   Mediator Worksheet with Teacher or Parent as Mediator

Target Student: Target Mediators:

What does/do mediator/s want/need?

What is/are mediator/s doing now and why?

How is it working to meet the student's need for behavior change?

How is it working to meet the mediator's needs now and in the future?

How can the intervention be changed to address both student and mediator needs?

The *Effort to Implement Scale* is used by behavioral consultants to guide decision making about whether or not a particular intervention approach is achievable for mediators (see Figure 5). Teachers, for example, have multiple demands on their time and attention in the classroom, so knowing whether an intervention can fit within that context is important or the teacher cannot implement with integrity the intervention suggested by a consultant. Use this scale to ascertain whether a particular recommended intervention approach is something you will actually be able to do—or not. If the intervention plan isn't a reasonable fit for your classroom, it won't be carried out as intended and the child won't have a fair chance of improving his or her behavior. Therefore, it is important for you, as the teacher, to be frank about your challenges in managing an entire classroom as well as responding to a particular child. Accordingly, the consultant specialist can then work constructively with you to identify an approach that you can and will implement rigorously.

Figure 5 Effort to Implement Scale

For each item below, rate the different aspects that require consideration if the intervention mediator is to implement the planned intervention, using the scale from 1 to 5 ranging from 1 as "low" effort to 5 as "high" effort based on your judgment regarding discrepancies between what now exists and what the intervention requires.

		Rating:				
		Low		**Average**		**High**
1.	Overall effort by the adult needed to implement the intervention	1	2	3	4	5
2.	Resources needed (time and materials) to implement the intervention	1	2	3	4	5
3.	The cultural fit of the intervention	1	2	3	4	5
4.	Technical skills needed to implement the intervention	1	2	3	4	5
5.	The match between personal values and the intervention procedure for the person who will intervene	1	2	3	4	5
6.	Perceptions by the interventionist that this plan is in the student's best interest	1	2	3	4	5

Source: Adapted with permission from Schindler and Horner (2005).

INTRODUCING THE FOUR-COMPONENT INTERVENTION MODEL

At this point, we contrast all these background conditions (strengths-based, barriers to change, cultural sensitivity, team work, and the role of mediators) with what can be thought of as the foreground—the actual intervention. Here we briefly provide a useful model for assembling all the necessary pieces of a comprehensive plan. The model is deceptively simple, in that it seems very obvious. Over a long period of development of behavioral interventions, each component of the model has been at one time or another extensively described and researched in the scientific literature. None of the four principles is rocket science. Nevertheless, in the literature one still finds examples involving the use of only one, or at most two, of these principles at any one time despite solid evidence that meaningful behavior change involves all four components.

Consider the first principle, often described as an ecological strategy—change the child's environment or remove triggers to inappropriate behavior. This sounds like a great idea: remove the things that provoke negative behavior and the negative behavior is reduced. A typical example in the early literature shows how far-fetched this approach can seem if applied in isolation. A possible explanation for self-stimulatory behavior in a child with autism, like tapping or banging on a desk, could be that it is the auditory feedback received by a child with autism that serves as reinforcement. Thus, it was suggested that all hard objects in the child's environment could be covered with foam rubber so there was no more reinforcing auditory feedback—obviously a wildly impractical intervention. Or consider the child who has a tantrum when presented with a difficult or unpleasant task? The ecological principle might be to never give the child an unpleasant task—again, a potentially useful idea, but life is unfortunately full of unpleasant tasks that we must do. In other words, a possibly valuable therapeutic principle cannot be used *alone* as a single-strategy intervention.

Clearly, what is needed is the *simultaneous* application of the four major ideas that emerge from behavioral and cognitive-behavioral psychology: the "four-component model" (Evans, 1989; Meyer & Evans, 1989). These four essential components needed for all Level 2 and Level 3 interventions can be described according to terms that are readily interpreted by professionals, families, specialists, and students alike:

1. **Prevent** (remove triggers and establish positive environments and social relationships that are culturally safe with clear expectations and supports for positive discipline)

2. **Educate** (teach alternative skills that are appropriate behaviors to replace challenging behaviors and that have greater acceptability and higher functional utility compared with the original problem behavior in the classroom, school, and community)

3. **Restore** (ensure that consequences for behavior are natural, including both positive and negative consequences which provide the student and others involved with the opportunity to restore relationships and preserve individual dignity and mutual respect)

4. **Think** (examine the underlying understandings, interpretations, and emotions surrounding behavioral expectations, events, and incidents held by the student as well as by mediators—teachers, peers, family members, and others who interact with the young person)

SUMMARY

We have presented the case that before specific intervention plans with individual students are implemented, there are certain important background factors to consider: the student's strengths, barriers to change, cultural identity, and working in a team that includes all relevant mediators. We then introduced a model for the intervention itself that proposes there are four components to an effective plan that must be carried out simultaneously. In the next chapter we elaborate on these four principles and provide more detailed examples of how they are implemented in the cases of three students at different stages of development—elementary school, middle school, and high school.

7 Interventions for Individual Students

Principles in Practice

Teachers are not expected to be responsible for the design of a total plan for responding to the most challenging student behaviors. But if you are aware of the principles used by behavioral and mental health consultants, it is easier for you to fit in with and follow their suggestions. There is the danger that an excellent, comprehensive, and detailed intervention plan can be put forward that actually relies in large part on strategies to be carried out by the child's teacher. This puts teachers in a difficult, if not impossible, situation. Instead, we advocate that plans are realistic and doable in the context of the daily responsibilities of a busy classroom teacher.

In this chapter, we elaborate on the PERT (prevent, educate, restore, think) model to explain more fully the above four components; we also give practical examples of how the components can be implemented for students at elementary, middle, and high school levels. We describe actual students but, of course, have changed their names and a few details to protect their privacy. We focus on those issues that are most relevant to teachers and expect that some of the components require really detailed plans whose implementation is the responsibility of the behavioral consultant. The third guide in this series is written for behavioral experts (these might be school psychologists, social workers, or counselors in your particular school system, or perhaps mental health professionals specifically designated as the behavioral consultant.) If you are interested in further details about treatment plans, this third guide book can be consulted.

PREVENT—ALTERING ANTECEDENT SETTINGS AND EVENTS

With the possible exception of neurological conditions like tics or seizures, children's problematic behaviors never just come out of the blue. Teachers sometimes say "he just suddenly snapped" or "her aggression was completely unprovoked," but what this really means is that we don't actually know what precipitated an emotionally charged outburst. We don't know what was going through the minds of the two students first described in Chapter 6 (what Nikotemo was thinking when he defecated on the floor rather than in the toilet, or what events preceded Jayla setting fire to the school hall). But we do know that something triggered these behaviors and we need more information in order to prevent reoccurrences in the future. Some triggers are immediately identifiable to the watchful eye, whereas others may be things that happened to the child when you were not around. Some precipitating events might have occurred much earlier in time—what behavioral psychologists call "setting events." Often triggers happen at home, for instance being in the midst of a domestic argument before coming to school, or being grounded for a week for forgetting to feed the cat. Some precipitating events are internal (private thoughts and feelings); only the child knows these, but hopefully will be able to explain and describe them to someone else.

Ecological Change

In traditional applied behavior analysis approaches to challenging behavior, teachers are encouraged to record "antecedents, behaviors, and consequences." This A-B-C analysis is very useful—always try to notice what happened just before the behavior, exactly what behavior occurred, and the consequences of the behavior. If your school has established good procedures for reporting incidents, an A-B-C log helps identify precipitating events or situations and interactions that typically lead to serious behavior incidents. This is why we often still refer to this component of the model as the "ecological" component. It *is* useful to think of environmental triggers because environments (contexts) can often be easily changed. Children with autism can be easily agitated by a loud or unpleasant noise; hot, clammy weather can make children irritable; boring, repetitive tasks can trigger escape behaviors. Often we can avoid or change these contexts: don't take the child with autism to a demolition derby; get an air-conditioner for the classroom; intersperse fun activities with the more tedious ones.

Just remember, however, the antecedent is not always an immediately observable, environmental event—an external stimulus of some kind—it might be an emotional, social, or psychological event. Many antecedents are social, emotional, or cognitive. An aggressive child might attack a peer who is laughing at him (or whom he thinks is laughing at him); feeling jealous of another student might make an insecure child act out for attention; ruminating about a past injustice may give a student thoughts of revenge, which can then trigger an act such as fire setting. Greene (2008) asserts that "most kids with behavioral challenges have five or six unresolved problems that are routinely precipitating their challenging episodes" (p. 75). He recommends that these precipitating problems should be resolved one by one so that in the future they no longer lead to challenging episodes.

Prevention

This first component is closely focused on deterrence and called "prevent" because a child's triggering events, situations, and interactions can be prevented from occurring in different environments and in the future. In fact, until the child acquires the skills and understandings needed to respond more adaptively to problematic antecedents, changing contexts (environments, settings, activities) is an important way of possibly reducing the probability of challenging behavior while other, slower-acting components of a new intervention are being put into place. For example Nikotemo's teacher Gayle noticed that many of his annoying classroom behaviors occurred during times when the work was difficult; he did not know the answers; and he was not putting up his hand or getting much attention from her. Originally she thought that he did not deserve attention until he behaved better, but then she understood that until he received some positive attention, he would *not* behave better! So she implemented a preventative, ecological daily strategy of identifying four to five areas where she could praise Nikotemo's responses or actions. At first the strategy was artificial, since she really had to struggle to find something praiseworthy, but soon there were positive events meriting genuine praise.

In the early stages of an intervention, it is crucial to avoid provocative, emotive antecedent events and negative situations altogether. This is because the student hasn't yet learned either the skills or cognitive controls to prevent negative behavior reactions that are now ingrained habits. In the early stages of acquiring new skills to react differently, it is easier and even tempting for the student to fall back on old habits. (Imagine you are trying to lose weight by eating less candy. Until you have acquired good self-control skills, an ecological, preventative strategy is to make sure you remove all candy from your house.) Gradually, the student is exposed to risky situations in order to practice new skills and develop fluency in using those new skills—rather than using older challenging behaviors. (Once you have committed to your weight loss plan, can exercise restraint, and no longer crave sweet things, you can easily pass up taking a chocolate, even if the box is handed to you.)

Ultimately, not all negative events associated with challenging behavior can be prevented from happening. The goal, however, is to try to at least prevent those that are the most negative from occurring while the educative components of the intervention plan are being mastered. When Jayla was interviewed in a supportive manner, she revealed that she smoked a joint with her friends mostly when she was feeling very tense and overwhelmed by her school work. Eventually, she had to learn to handle academic demands as well as pressure from her friends, but until she had worked out a plan to better manage her homework, test preparation, and general study, as well as being able to resist pressure from her friends without fear of rejection, all her subject teachers agreed to give her a little less work, back off on some demands, and extend some deadlines just for the rest of the semester. This student urgently needed to acquire new, adaptive skills and understandings to respond to the inevitable ups and downs and pressures of real life. But until then, in the early stages of an intervention plan, students like Jayla with social, emotional, and behavior challenges that they cannot handle should receive additional support from adults and peers who can prevent and mediate conflict and confrontations.

EDUCATE—TEACHING POSITIVE REPLACEMENT SKILLS

Old-fashioned behavior management practices were based almost exclusively on the sole application of the principles of reinforcement. Good behavior was to be rewarded, which in turn would lead to increases in that behavior. Undesired behavior should not be rewarded (extinguished through ignoring) or even followed by punishment to decrease that behavior. Unfortunately, this simple formula doesn't specify what the child should do when he or she doesn't have any positive alternative skills (e.g., negotiation), but is perfectly competent in negative behavior (e.g., fighting) that does in fact achieve the desired results (i.e., the rewarding object or experience) for the child at least some of the time. Thus, a crucial step in the intervention process is to identify the skills that the students need to learn and then teach them to use these as replacements for highly inappropriate behavior.

Replacement Skills Should Serve the Same Function

Information about the sequence of events associated with a child's negative behavior provides valuable clues about the purpose, or *function*, of the behavior. What is the student trying to achieve? What outcome or benefit is maintaining the behavior we judge as undesirable? Is it really undesirable from the child's point of view?

For example, if a student is continuously referred to the office by one or more teachers for disruptive classroom behavior, it is important to know more about what happened in order to figure out the likely function. The goal of a restorative approach is not to simply punish the student, but instead to try to prevent similar incidents from happening in the future. Some negative behavior serves the function of impressing peers or maintaining one's social standing. Without identifying the potential harm that is done and subsequently using restorative practices to make amends, the student is not given the opportunity nor expected to make things right but instead is actually encouraged to continue to be disruptive lest he lose face in front of others.

The activity included here presents a typical scenario likely to lead to an office referral in middle school and illustrates how everyone in the room becomes locked into a negative interaction pattern that almost appears to instigate escalation rather than diminishing the problem and starting anew (see insert). As you review the scenario, keep in mind that both the teacher and classmates could have chosen to engage in various replacement behaviors that might have affected Samuel's behavior differently. Furthermore, a crucial point to review is whether or not Samuel actually has the skills needed to behave any differently than he did. What do you think?

Activity: Review the following sequence of events in a math class that ended with Samuel being referred to the office. For each step in the sequence, identify a possible alternative skill scenario that might have occurred that could have replaced the negative antecedents and behaviors that actually happened.

What happened	Possible alternative skill scenario
The teacher tells students to review briefly the pages assigned as math homework the night before and independently complete a worksheet she has handed out to assess their understanding.	
Samuel didn't read the pages in the textbook assigned by the teacher the night before, and he also doesn't have a pencil with him.	

(Continued)

(Continued)

What happened	Possible alternative skill scenario
Samuel raises his hand and loudly asks the teacher for a pencil, which she gives him while commenting that this is the fifth pencil she has given him that month.	
Samuel doesn't know any of the answers so starts to draw graffiti-type scribbles on his worksheet.	
Students seated on either side of Samuel start to laugh, and Samuel says loudly, "What are you laughing at, you #@*%&ers!"	
The teacher looks up and says, "Samuel, quiet!"	
Samuel growls but starts drawing again, pushing hard on the pencil so that the lead breaks.	
Samuel gets out of his seat and walks to the pencil sharpener where he makes quite a show of things, then taps several desks with the tip of his pencil while walking back to his seat.	
A student mutters "Stop that, you jerk!" in a low voice that the teacher doesn't hear.	
Samuel says loudly, "Why should I, loser?"	
The teacher hears this and says loudly, "Samuel, don't make me have to tell you again!"	
Samuel smiles defiantly and says, "Or you'll do *what* to me?"	

A negative pattern such as this one between the teacher and a student can become so entrenched that the act of being sent to the office, intended as "punishment," becomes "reinforcement" for both the teacher and the student. The teacher can be forgiven for thinking that the rest of the class period will go better once Samuel leaves the room. And Samuel may consider it worth it to avoid doing the math worksheet and having to reveal to everyone that he cannot, in fact, answer the questions. Worse, in the long run, the only way to prevent future occurrences of the above behavior pattern may be construed by everyone as achievable only by the permanent exclusion of Samuel from the class.

Appropriate Alternatives

For Nikotemo, the Samoan boy discussed earlier, simulating masturbation at the age of 8 is unlikely to be a specific sexual act and neither is exposing himself; it is more probable that Nikotemo discovered these were a sure-fire way to gain attention and shock both his peers and his teachers. And it worked rather well—there was much more consternation in the school regarding this action and his sexually explicit comments than almost anything else he did. Aveolela found it very difficult to talk about this in the group meeting; it was obvious she felt shame. But because she could now confide in Gayle, she was able to explain that she thought sex was something dirty, so she had done her best to shield Nikotemo from all mention of the topic—indeed, she could not understand where he had learned such things. Gayle quietly explained the influence of TV, the Internet, the neighborhood kids, and suggested that Aveolela, perhaps with help of a male Sunday school teacher at her church (whom she liked), start to address sexuality issues frankly and matter-of-factly with Nikotemo, emphasizing what was normal, what was private, and other social rules around sexual expression.

There might be a related function to some of Nikotemo's other behaviors. During class time, the triggers for Nikotemo's disruptive behavior were feeling unappreciated (lack of attention), but they were also when the work was hard for him and he felt anxious and confused. Now, if you are given a job by your principal that seems a bit beyond your training or experience, what do you do? You won't tip over the principal's box of pens or throw a water bottle at her. Instead, a professional adult knows how to say politely that assistance or further professional development is needed before taking on such a complex task. Gayle realized that Nikotemo simply did not know how to ask for help (or felt dumb when he did, and so he often said the work was dumb). She taught him and the rest of the class some strategies for tackling new problems, such as talking to oneself: "Hmm, let's see, what do I have to do here? What do I know about this sort of problem? Take my time; I can figure it out. If not, there's no shame in asking for help." (The exact words of these meta-cognitive, self-talk strategies are not important—you will select the language suitable for the developmental level and cultural styles of the student. The important thing is to teach the child to legitimize asking for help after first attempting to complete the task.)

Interestingly, Jayla's behavior at school also often seemed to serve the function of escape from difficult task demands. She had changed schools often and so was behind on the curriculum, a fact not always realized by her teachers who knew she was bright. But, in reaching 10th grade, she was now faced with academic work substantially more difficult than previously encountered, work that relied more on background knowledge. Jayla also had to learn some skills for dealing with the stress of adolescence that were a bit more adaptive than smoking dope or swearing at teachers. So the school counselor set up a few sessions with her and a couple of other struggling students; she called the program "Coping

Cats—how you cope with bad feelings without getting out your claws." (The counselor borrowed the program and the ideas from *Coping Cat©*, a program for anxious children and youth developed by Kendall and Hedtke, 2006.)

RESTORE—CONSEQUENCES, NOT RETRIBUTION

Restorative school discipline does not mean that there are no consequences for behavior. There are natural consequences for negative behavior, and part of the purpose of schooling is to educate young people about expectations for their behavior as well as what will happen when they fail to meet those expectations. However natural and logical those consequences for negative behavior might be, consequences that do no more than punish the offender accomplish little or nothing towards fixing damage or harm that may have resulted from the behavioral incident.

Consequences such as suspension and exclusion may have the desired (by some) effect of temporarily separating offenders from victims but, again, this is only a temporary solution unless amends are made to the satisfaction of all parties. Theoretically, suspension and removal from a negative situation provides participants opportunity to reflect on events, away from provocation or negative feelings. But in reality, removal from the situation can also operate as reinforcement as the problem temporarily "goes away" and, meanwhile, negative attributions may actually escalate as each participant nurtures hostile interpretations of events rather than exploring alternative interpretations that could heal relationships. Finally, punishment that is for the sole purpose of retribution is really more appropriate for criminal offenses than it is for use in an educational context. The major purpose of an educational system and of schools is to educate young people to become productive citizens. Unless a crime has been committed resulting in legal action from the criminal justice system, schools should remain true to their educational purpose to educate and be educative.

Natural Consequences

Restore, the third component of effective interventions, is, therefore, designed to ensure that consequences for behavior are supportive in providing opportunities for the restoration of relationships through mutual respect and the preservation of individual dignity. Offenders and victims alike have the right to have their voices heard, and it is important that they hear one another's perceptions of events with the intent of understanding what is needed to make amends and move forward. Review the scenario for Samuel on pages 103–104. Even where there isn't really a "victim," as in this instance, a great deal can be done towards restoration of what appears to be damaged relationships between Samuel, his peers, and his teacher. Describe a mediation process—it could be shuttle mediation (see Chapter 5)—that can be used to restore these relationships rather than punishments that, in fact, can increase Samuel's hostility towards the teacher and some of his classmates. Any consequences that are delivered to Samuel for his behavior have to be consistent with current class rules, but until Samuel has the necessary skills to stop a negative chain such as this from occurring, it is up to the teacher and other school personnel to act.

In any school, there needs to be agreement and consistency regarding the consequences for negative behavior. For example, where school expectations include coming to class with needed materials, including pens, calculators, and textbooks, it is problematic to have a range of possible consequences for an infraction applied idiosyncratically by different teachers, with different students, at different times. Delivering a gentle verbal reminder to Melissa on Monday for forgetting her pencil but reprimanding Samuel sternly in a negative tone of voice on Tuesday for the same issue is perceived by students as differential treatment; Samuel, in particular, is going to feel that he has been treated unfairly. We have seen school lists of a wide range of possible consequences for bringing cell phones or iPods to class, ranging from a temporary confiscation of the item, to returning the item at the end of the semester, or not at all, without any specificity regarding which of these will apply in any given instance. This creates considerable potential for feelings of discrimination and favoritism as well as perceptions of being treated unfairly based on whether or not a particular teacher is singling out particular students. Particularly because this is the kind of "violation" that can be predicted and is likely to occur, it should be easy to reach consensus across school personnel about consistent, transparent, and fair application of consequences for transgressions—it should not be left to the whim of the moment.

Safety Considerations

Where transgressions are more serious and actual harm has occurred or been threatened, there is still the need to redress that harm in a way that does not strip people of their dignity in a manner that makes future recovery impossible. We need to put a stop to a dangerous behavior, but it must be addressed in a proactive way. Children who are backed into a corner save face by becoming more and more aggressive rather than lose what they see as the only remaining power they can exercise—defiance. By the time violence has occurred, responding in kind only aggravates and increases hostilities for everyone. At that point, safety for everyone is paramount but attaining this security does not have to be at the expense of long-term relationships. The process for a formal restorative conference provides a structure to respond to serious behavior that has harmed or threatened to harm others, and in-school suspension provides a safe environment for the healing process to begin consistent with restorative school discipline (see Chapter 8).

In our interwoven case examples, there are two acts that had to be dealt with firmly without escalation potential. Nikotemo's defecating on the toilet floor resulted in huge excitement across the school. Gayle had to persuade the principal not to make a new school rule about toilet use. She argued that it was a unique event, causes unknown, that was not likely to be repeated. But a few weeks later a "keep our school tidy" plan was promulgated in which there was an emphasis on using the trashcans, cleaning up your own mess after lunch, picking up litter, and recycling. Nikotemo was quietly encouraged to be active in this new campaign and his mother was asked to make sure that he learned to be responsible for clearing up after himself at home—Aveolela was a bit over-indulgent and did not expect her two boys to do any household chores.

Jayla's fire setting was substantially more serious, and she and the school were extremely lucky that it caused only minor damage. While the expulsion process was placed in abeyance under the restorative principles, the school leaders were determined that serious consequences had to result. During the restorative meetings, Jayla came to recognize the harm she had caused and the potential threat to many people, including her friends. She was required to pay for the damage by working at the school after hours, and she lost various privileges at home and was grounded for a period of time. She was required to write a letter of apology to the local fire department who had responded to the emergency call. There are many alternative possibilities. You might be able to think of other socially appropriate consequences that would not humiliate her or make her even more deeply resentful.

THINK—TEACHING NEW UNDERSTANDINGS AND EMOTIONAL SKILLS

In addition to learning new skills and practicing positive adaptive behaviors, students with challenging behavior are likely to have distorted underlying understandings, interpretations, and emotions about events, circumstances, and even their relationships with other people. Greene (2008) emphasizes that children with challenging behavior and who have social and emotional problems lack "important thinking skills" (p. 10). In association with ongoing conflict at home and in school, there may also be some truth to a child's perceptions of rejection and hostility from others—teachers, peers, family members, and others who interact with the young person. After all, when teachers start to feel they have been treated badly by a child after genuine attempts to help and offer support, they may show an exaggerated negative response to challenging behavior. This can be detected by the student, confirming his or her view that people are unfair and always on their case. It is important to acknowledge that negative interaction patterns are likely to have become established in interactions with others at school, and that the child perceives that others don't care, dislike him or her, or even feels that others are "out to get him."

Cognitive and Emotional Distortions

Contemporary cognitive behavior therapy (CBT) approaches to interventions address not only the observable skills and behaviors that become new actions, but also the thinking behind events and behaviors. Young people diagnosed as having severe conduct disorders not only demonstrate negative acting-out behavior that is harmful to others, they also perceive hostile intent in the actions of others. Interpretations of hostile intent mean that a perfectly innocent mistake such as bumping into someone in the school corridor is incorrectly judged as a deliberate act intended to cause harm, embarrassment, or disrespect. Children who ascribe hostile intent to the acts of others, as almost their default interpretation, require interventions that focus on both new skills and understandings about behavior—how they think about events and circumstances.

In Jayla's case, it was discovered that the fire-setting incidents were precipitated by lengthy periods of revenge fantasies that she had regarding a series of what she considered injustices by the school staff. On one occasion, after she had been sent to the Deputy Principal by a class teacher, he gave her a long lecture on being more mature and responsible. Some of our teacher colleagues encourage what they call "the two-sentence rule" in which you do not reprimand a student for more than two sentences. As one teacher said to us:

> When disciplining a child two sentences are enough. The kid knows they've done wrong, and if you say anything more than that you see the resentment build up in their eyes. So why do some teachers keep going on and on and on and on? You can see that kid's face change from "I'm sorry" to "I can't stand you." Why do teachers do it? (Evans & Harvey, 2012)

And so it was that Jayla left that meeting not feeling remorse for what she knew she had done wrong, but feeling resentful, and she spent a considerable amount of fantasy time thinking how she could get back at the DP. These are not constructive feelings, as we all know. Accepting responsibility for our actions, accepting criticism, and making amends rather than getting revenge are all parts of emotional intelligence. Jayla lacked these emotion competencies.

It became clear that counseling focused on Jayla's understanding of her own feelings was needed. But counseling can be artificial for a student like Jayla. Instead, we thought, what if we could get her some formal guitar lessons with a gifted music teacher? Such a person might be able to interest her in the feelings and messages of many popular and classic songs and ballads. Music and song lyrics are very salient sources of emotional information to teenagers. And what if we could find such a person who was also African American, totally comfortable with his or her identity as a gifted black person? This approach builds on Jayla's strengths, provides a role model helping her clarify her ethnic and cultural identity, and encourages natural learning opportunities. It is an excellent example of using a natural support person not as a therapist, but as a mediator, as a mentor.

EXAMPLES OF THE FOUR-COMPONENT MODEL IN ACTION

An Elementary School Student Example: Justin

Justin is 7 years of age and is repeating the first grade. He was held back because his first-grade teacher seemed to manage his behavior very successfully. However, her husband was offered a new position on the other coast and she resigned early in the school year. The new teacher, Mr. Cartwright, is quite inexperienced but emphasizes an upbeat class atmosphere with clear rules, plenty of structure, reliable routines, and high expectations. Justin did not handle the change at all well and reverted to a pattern of negative behaviors he exemplified in kindergarten: he was described by Mr. Cartwright as having an extremely poor attention span, refusing to sit still (often wandering about the room), and noncompliant. If asked to change from one activity to another, Justin often had a major tantrum, throwing himself on the floor and screaming. These episodes could last a long time and Mr. Cartwright felt compelled, when they occurred, to call Justin's mother, who is a dental nurse, to come to the school to collect him.

Justin has been diagnosed with autism. Although his parents, George and Beth, believe he is high functioning, the pediatric assessments completed when he was 4 noted very limited communication skills (he has an extensive labeling vocabulary but is deficient in carrying on an interactive conversation) and his play seems largely self-stimulatory and ritualistic. He has few self-care skills although he can dress himself, eats with a spoon, and is toilet trained. Justin is agile and athletic; he climbs trees with no apparent concern for safety and has to be watched constantly around traffic as he is quite capable of darting out across the street if he sees something of interest, usually shiny objects that he will then hold in his hand for a long period of time. Mr. Cartwright is most frustrated by Justin's consistent refusal to follow commands, inability to sit still, and his extreme tantrums. Because of these concerns, Justin's parents have sought further medical advice and Justin is currently taking the antipsychotic medication Risperidone (1 mg in the morning and 1.5 mg at bedtime). According to George, his father, the medicine has a somewhat positive effect on his random activity, although his mother Beth worries about him seeming more listless (sedated), and his noncompliance at school remains unimproved.

There is tension between the school and Justin's parents: (a) George and Beth, who did not agree on the use of drugs, were exploring a private provider of intensive "ABA" services (applied behavior analysis procedures following the Lovaas method, a highly structured program that relies heavily on discrete trial training methods (Lovaas, 1981); (b) they were involved with psychiatric services monitoring medication the doctor believed was essential; (c) Beth was angry with the school about being called at work to collect Justin whenever he was out of control; (d) they were not convinced of the adequacy of the training of a full-time teacher aide whom the school principal had decided was needed to shadow Justin in the classroom. As a result, there was an urgent need for a restorative-style meeting to bring all parties together to work within a comprehensive plan. However, Mr. Cartwright felt he did not want to wait for that to happen and said he would like to design a simple four-component plan that he could implement in his classroom immediately. After talking with the school psychologist, the following strategies were tried simultaneously with Justin.

Prevent

Mr. Cartwright had been keeping notes on Justin's tantrums and saw that there were two major antecedent conditions: a change in routine or being asked to stop a task he was engrossed in; and the introduction of a new classroom activity that was not one of Justin's skill areas. He decided to give Justin only his favorite activities for a period of time. He selected useful classroom activities that he knew Justin typically completed successfully. To make it seem fair to all the other children he introduced periods during the day called "Reflection," in which the class were allowed to go back over things they had already learned, thus ensuring a high level of success (and engagement) for everyone. Mr. Cartwright remembered an article he had read during his training about an approach called "gentle teaching" (McGee, Menolascino, Hobbs, & Menousek, 1987) and thought he'd give it a try. This approach is a bit like errorless learning, in that the child controls the interactions with the teacher, makes choices, and shows what he is interested in or wants to do. The student directs and the teacher follows, a little bit like you might play with a toddler. The goal is for the child to feel safe, engaged, and unconditionally valued. The school psychologist joked with him and said "you've changed from being a fairly warm demander to being a very warm non-demander!"

Changing from one activity to another was a bit harder because Mr. Cartwright felt he couldn't let Justin just do the same activity all the time when the class activities had to change—there had to be some demands placed on Justin. He realized that he needed a teaching strategy for this and decided to use "social stories," which we will explain in the next section. But as an attempt to prepare Justin for transitions he designed a visual "timetable" depicting the main activities of the day (class greeting on the mat, music, recess, math, science project outside—those sort of large categories requiring change in location as well as activity). First thing in the morning Mr. Cartwright rehearsed the day's routines with Justin and also started giving him "5-minute, 2-minute, time!" warnings prior to a transition; he noticed that quite a few other students benefited from these cues as well, since many of them hated stopping an activity they were deeply involved with.

Educate

The school psychologist directed Mr. Cartwright to an article by Carr and Durand (1985), which suggested that very often the function of disruptive and tantrum behavior is to communicate that the student wants some object, doesn't want something (desire to escape), is bored, or desires attention. Thus, the best alternatives to teach are simple communication skills, either vocal or using signs and pointing to pictures. Although this is an excellent approach, Mr. Cartwright realized that it requires a long-term initiative involving the district's speech/language therapist. So while that was being established, he focused on two alternative skill approaches: social stories and self-calming strategies.

Social stories is a technique developed by Carol Gray (1993). A social story is written in the first person from the perspective of the child, giving as much information as possible about what is expected, where, why, and who is involved. Children's own words and thoughts are used, if they can be. In Justin's case, other students were asked to help illustrate each social story—some of them were really good at drawing, and this was more constructive than Mr. Cartwright's usual instruction to the rest of the class, which was "Class, just ignore Justin right now; he is being disrespectful of our class rules; we're not going to pay any attention to him." (This kind of statement of course separated Justin as the deviant child, not one of "us.")

A sample social story to help Justin learn classroom rules is as follows:

Justin's Wait-Until-Recess Story

*Some things we do in first grade * have to be done seated at a table.*

Sometimes I hate to sit down and I get up and run around. This bothers my friends.

*So when I feel like running I must try to wait for recess *.*

*The other kids at my table are happy * when I sit quietly with them and help my group *.*

(Where we have inserted asterisks, small pictures were added: a photo of the classroom door, a drawing of the kids running around during recess, a whole lot of smiley faces, and a photo, taken by Mr. Cartwright, of Justin working with his group.)

Another crucial area for Justin to develop alternative skills is for him to understand his own feelings and the feelings of others—one of the critical needs that we now know characterizes children with autistic spectrum disorders (ASD). There are many good programs that developed around this theme (e.g., Howlin, Baron-Cohen, & Hadwin, 1999). But this too is a rather specialized long-term strategy; Mr. Cartwright thought he'd bring it up at the restorative planning meeting, but in terms of what he realistically could do in a regular classroom with 27 other students to worry about, he decided on a simpler plan for now. This was to teach everyone in the class, including Justin, two simple techniques to manage frustration, anger, and overexcitement. One is to take a big breath, blow out your cheeks, and then very slowly let all the air out of the "balloon" in your mouth. During class practice, some of the more boisterous boys went red in the face with holding their breath and then let it out with a great burst of air and spit; they had to be told not to be so silly and to follow Justin, who knew how to do it very slowly. The second technique referenced the popular cartoon character Sponge Bob in training the kids in simple relaxation techniques, that is, letting your muscles go all squishy like a sponge. There is an extensive research literature on the value of teaching stress-management and coping strategies to children with autism (Baron, Groden, Groden, & Lipsitt, 2006).

Restore

Remember this is the component when natural—and agreed-upon—consequences for behavior are decided. Since the new plan was not going to instantly solve all the problems, Mr. Cartwright realized the biggest issue was how to provide a nonpunitive consequence for Justin when he has a major meltdown tantrum. As Justin's safety and the safety of the other students is paramount, the social worker attached to this elementary school was enlisted to help. The plan they came up with was that Mr. Cartwright would text her on his cell phone if a temper outburst had gone out of control. She would drop whatever she was doing, come to the classroom, and carefully but firmly escort Justin to a small room near the school office, sometimes used by the principal for parent meetings. In the room was a selection of workbooks which could distract Justin, once he had settled down. His mother Beth would be texted at the same time, but just for information—she was not asked to come to the school. Once Justin calmed down, and only then, the social worker (or any other adult in the office if she could not stay that long) could start to interact positively with Justin, direct him to the workbooks, and remind him in only two calm sentences why the tantrum behavior was unacceptable—to his teacher, his peers, and the school. When returned to the classroom Justin was encouraged to say sorry to Mr. Cartwright, but this was not insisted upon.

Think

Justin was much less of a problem during the previous year because his teacher that year pretty much let him do whatever he wanted. That could not really go on, despite Mr. Cartwright's new ecological strategy of greatly reducing demands for immediate compliance. What was wanted was that Justin would be motivated to fit in, behave like the other children (imitate them), and see himself as part of the class. Mr. Cartwright knew these important social-emotional skills and increased cognitive understanding take a long time to acquire for a child with significant autism. But to make a start he invited a couple of the more mature students to agree to spend a little time with Justin during recess, lunchtime, and while waiting for his transport home (Justin could not yet be trusted on the buses and went home each day in a taxi). Mr. Cartwright gave this group of "special friends" some suggestions, but little formal direction: "Let Justin show you his electronic game; show him how to take turns; see if he'll kick a soccer ball back to you; challenge him to race—he'll probably beat you!; if he does something you don't like, tell him to stop—if he doesn't walk away. Remember he's just as much a member of this class as you guys are."

Did all this work? Bits of it did. Once fewer demands were being placed on Justin, tantrums essentially disappeared for a while. He had some trouble understanding the social stories idea, but the class got into it and started to want some stories personalized for all of them as well. To begin with, most of the first graders couldn't read their stories but they remembered them by heart. The special friends group acted rather officiously at first, like they had a new pet puppy; Mr. Cartwright had to remind them about respect and fairness. Beth started to come to the school without being ordered to, and Mr. Cartwright said it was fine if she wanted to pop in anytime; he noticed she was now a lot more cuddly with Justin. At the big restorative planning meeting two months later, Beth told the group that Mr. Cartwright was the perfect teacher for Justin.

A Middle School Student Example: Dilbert

Dilbert is 13 and in the eighth grade of a large suburban middle school in Colorado. He lives with his father and 16-year-old sister. His sister was expelled from the local high school for violent behavior and has not returned to school. She has a part-time job as a waitress at a café. Dilbert's mother was removed from the children's care by child protective services. She was a harsh and abusive parent with a drinking problem; even so, Dilbert misses her and is angry that he is not allowed contact. Dilbert's father is a salesman who spent many days and weeks on the road when the children were young. He is now forced to work from the company office, which is less productive. He resents being the sole care-giving parent but wants nothing to do with his wife.

Various behaviors, some of which have been problematic since second grade, led to involvement of the behavior support team. Dilbert is abusive and disrespectful if reprimanded, disruptive and noisy in class; he has been caught sending sexually explicit text messages. He was recently suspended for running his hand up a girl student's thigh. A psychological assessment completed the previous year described him as having "psychopathic traits" with little empathy for others, callous attitudes towards peers, and an ability to use superficial charm to get what he wants. He tested as having a high intelligence (full scale score of 129 on the Wechsler Intelligence Scale for Children) but is behind academically. He has no close friends at school. His father is described as cooperative, but seems emotionally distant and uninvolved. The psychologist is of the opinion that Dilbert spends too much time in the company of his sister and her 22-year-old boyfriend.

Determined to follow a restorative discipline approach, the team felt it was important to start with a clean slate and to encourage Dilbert to talk more about what sorts of things he wants in his life and what he might be able to achieve at school. A new series of interviews was initiated called "Dilbert Dreaming." He was asked to explain what he understood about his own behavior, what he most enjoyed doing with his dad, whether there were any other relatives he liked that might serve as role models or mentors. When told the intervention plan had to have ideas representing his own wishes, he said he wanted his mom involved and this was cleared with the family court. He admitted to being lonely, not having friends, and said he felt "stupid" in class as he was always behind the others. The boys he admired at school went snowboarding on weekends; he would like to do that, but his dad wouldn't let him. He said his life "sucked."

What might be referred to as "safety needs" were paramount in this case. The parents of the girl who was inappropriately touched were angry and talking to both police and the district superintendent. There was a danger that the response to the sexual offense, although serious, would be out of proportion to the nature of the offense; this reaction is sometimes referred to as moral panic. Juvenile sexual offending is very different from adult offending, but often is treated in much the same way (Zimring, 2004). Sexual offending by youth has a low recidivism rate (National Juvenile Justice Network, 2007). Nevertheless, it was important for Dilbert's protection as well as that of other students, to have a safety plan in place that consisted of the following agreed-upon conditions:

- Increase father's supervision at home to ensure Dilbert is not left alone with his sister
- Construct a clear action plan regarding consequences if he sexually assaults any other student again (excluding suspension)
- Dilbert agrees that his father can monitor his cell phone use—any inappropriate text messages results in loss of the cell phone
- Dilbert will not be referred to the Juvenile Justice service
- The involved girl's parents will discuss the issue with her in a calm, neutral manner

At this point there was agreement that those remaining involved in Dilbert's intervention plan should be his father, his mother, the school counselor, his English teacher (whom he really likes and who has taken an interest in him), the deputy principal, and Dilbert's uncle (whom he nominated as someone he trusts). His uncle is a lab technician at the nearby university.

Prevent

His English teacher arranged for him to have *additional* work and assignments to "help him catch up." The message was that as a "warm, demanding teacher," she had expectations regarding his ability to achieve. Dilbert could also stop by the DP's office if he had some positive experience to recount, or just felt the need to talk.

Educate

The school counselor agreed to work through the "moral reasoning" (empathy) training sections of Goldstein, Glick, and Gibb's (1998) Aggression Replacement Training (ART). This part of the ART manual increases students' understanding of fairness, justice, and concern for the needs and rights of others, through the use of exercises and scenarios presenting moral reasoning dilemmas. The health education teacher agreed to conduct some special sessions for Dilbert's entire class on the importance of relationships and the natural developmental changes regarding sexuality in adolescent boys and girls (without reference to any incident or any student).

Restore

His father agreed to Dilbert receiving coaching in snowboarding and arranged regular visits to the Eldora Ski Resort; Dilbert's mother agreed to pay as long as he continued to get favorable reports from the school regarding his behavior. His English teacher worked with him on writing a humorous essay on learning to snowboard for the school magazine; his uncle was assigned the task of taking some photos of Dilbert's efforts and showing him how to put them on a Facebook page. The DP agreed to find a group of boys in the school who were also beginners so that they could sometimes go to Eldora together to practice snowboarding.

Think

The team asked the school counselor, with Dilbert's agreement, to explore his anger regarding his mother. The counselor also suggested working with the snowboarding coach to find out what rules and skills regarding self-control, safety, and concern for others were considered important when on a ski slope. These would be used as examples for Dilbert of how to be more mature and responsible regarding the needs of others. Dilbert was encouraged to ask for help from his English teacher or the DP, as well as his uncle, when he found academic work challenging rather than dismissing the work as unimportant.

Although this was a complex plan, the demands on any one individual mediator's time or skills was not that great. As long as each person in the team knew and accepted their roles and worked together with one another, the plan had many positive features. Dilbert's mother found her role difficult; her alcoholism caused some problems with follow-through, and Dilbert's father was not very accepting of her involvement. However, the counselor was able to help Dilbert understand some of the mother's emotional needs, and Dilbert became more accepting of her failings. The little group of boys who went snowboarding together formed some good peer relationships, although Dilbert was not as skilled as the others, who had been snowboarding for longer. For a while, Dilbert tried to impress them with some daredevil moves, but he twisted an ankle and started to talk more honestly with his friends about his limits, not needing to compete all the time, becoming more respectful of the other boys' prowess—admiring them without acting jealous. An interesting, slightly self-deprecating story about learning to snowboard appeared in his middle school's newspaper. Dilbert's spelling and grammar were checked by his English teacher, with whom he was getting on well. Other teachers referred Dilbert to the DP on four occasions after the plan went into effect, but the DP reported the incidents were minor and generally seem to have been started by other students.

A High School Student Example: Fernanda

Fernanda attends an inner-city high school in New Jersey. Her mother, Christina, and her father, Luis, came from Mexico as young adults and own a small convenience store. They are described by the social worker at a community mental health center as a respectable, hardworking couple with four children, and Fernanda, at 15, is their oldest. Historically, Fernanda has struggled academically at school and in elementary school was diagnosed with a specific learning disability (dyslexia). Her parents have always had a hard time controlling her, saying she has been defiant ever since they can remember, does not respect authority, steals money, has refused to attend the local church, and has fallen into the wrong crowd at school. Her father describes her as "a little shit." Recent, severe incidents at school resulted in an upcoming hearing, possibly leading to expulsion. The family was advised to seek psychiatric help and they have been referred to the mental health outpatient clinic of a public hospital in Newark.

The problems reported at school were described as follows:

- Picking fights by threatening and goading, with derogatory comments about other girls

- Physical intimidation—tripping, pushing, thumping others; threatening or standover tactics
- Defiance of authority—swearing and talking back
- Vandalism
- Violent, unprovoked physical aggression—kicking, punching

Fernanda hangs with a group of boys who are thought to be recruits for the Latin Kings, a violent street gang active in the neighborhood. The school denies they have a gang presence, but the boys she spends time with have been seen to sport the gang's colors of black and gold. Other students are frightened of her. Her teachers say she is unable to manage the conventional demands of the school day and that she is often absent without cause. Fernanda is a large, slightly overweight girl with a tattoo of a crown on her left shoulder. She is constantly in trouble with the dean of students at the school, who has stated that she does not belong in the school and should be in a juvenile detention facility. Basically no one has a good word for Fernanda.

The first restorative discipline meeting organized by the principal and the dean was somewhat confusing. In addition to the principal and dean, Christina and Luis were present and supported by their parish priest. There was a psychologist and a social worker from the adolescent mental health service, her homeroom teacher, a special education teacher, the school psychologist, a police youth aid officer, and a behavior specialist from the school district. Fernanda came to the meeting looking very agitated, but left after a few minutes, slamming the door behind her. Her mother looked embarrassed; her father muttered *tipico*, "typical," to no one in particular.

The special education teacher, Celia, and the behavior specialist, Gordon, were determined to focus on positive solutions and managed to elicit from the group, somewhat reluctantly, the following positive strengths:

- Fernanda did not seem to be sexually active and had no intimate boyfriend; she seemed cautious about sexually transmitted diseases or getting pregnant.
- Although often truant she did generally come to school and attend her classes.
- At the mental health clinic she had broken down in tears during an interview, saying everyone hated her. Being depressed or suicidal are not strengths, but the behavior indicated to the group that she was more vulnerable than she appeared, which might explain some of her aggression.

- She loved her younger siblings and was never aggressive with them. She was fairly close to her maternal grandmother, who spoke no English, and Fernanda had expressed interest in learning Spanish.
- She was in good physical health.
- Although the Latin Kings were known for drug dealing, it did not appear that Fernanda was involved with drugs.
- She had told her special education teacher she'd like to be a hairdresser.

This was not much for the team to work with, but there was a renewed sense of purpose in the group, a commitment to work together, and a sense that although this was really Fernanda's last chance, there was a possibility of turning this young person's life around. Celia and Gordon worked together to design the initial four-component plan.

Prevent

As Gordon had no prior history of working with Fernanda, and as Celia was probably the teacher she hated the least, they decided to really try to connect with her at her level. Short meetings were scheduled during class times; Fernanda enjoyed this opportunity to avoid "boring" classes. Discussion was focused entirely on establishing a meaningful therapeutic relationship with her. She was never criticized or reprimanded; Gordon tried to follow the principles of unconditional acceptance that are used in some forms of therapy, such as dialectical behavior therapy (DBT). The goal of this relationship building was to give her a sense of self-efficacy, acknowledging that she was now of an age where she could partially control her own destiny.

To build on that idea, Gordon and Celia's second strategy was to use a technique called "motivational interviewing" in which the goal is to allow the client to see that in order to achieve her own goals she has to make some behavioral changes. The carrot they dangled in front of Fernanda was that when she turned 16 that could be her last school year. (Obtaining agreement from her parents for this took some effort, as they thought very traditionally that education was the ticket to happiness and prosperity—one reason they were constantly berating her for poor school performance.) The school would ensure that she was awarded a Certificate of Completion, but that might exclude her from going to beauty school. Celia and Fernanda together searched for private hairdressing academies in the Newark area that would accept a 16-year-old without a high school diploma or GED. They found two. Luis promised to pay the necessary tuition fees if Fernanda could meet certain behavioral goals, specified under the *Restore* part of the plan.

This latter point shows how the various components are actually inter-related, not isolated elements of an intervention plan. Gordon and Celia saw the strategy of holding out some kind of meaningful future for Fernanda as an ecological and preventative procedure: without some sense of a future goal, there was nothing to motivate a rebellious teenager. Equally importantly, this strategy immediately resulted in a reduction in academic pressure. The school felt this was "giving in" to a manipulative student, but the reality was that Fernanda wasn't learning much at school anyway—deciding she could leave school at 16 allowed everyone working with her to reduce their incessant performance demands. This also meant that her remaining time in school would be more positive so that rather than accumulating two to three more years of failure in school, she could move on with some experiences of success. Leaving school with a more positive frame of mind could give her a sense of controlling her own destiny so that she might actually choose to study for the GED later, when things were going better for her. The new school-related demands were not academic: she had to come to school on time, attend classes or go to alternative classes organized by the special education department, obey school rules, and be respectful to all teachers.

Educate

Fernanda had so many negative behaviors it was difficult to generate alternative skills. However, during the interview sessions, Gordon and Celia probed to discover the function of her aggressive, bullying, and threatening behavior. There seemed to be a few basic functions. One was that these behaviors made her feel powerful—she liked the fact that other students were scared of her. Second, she believed that these behaviors ensured acceptance and respect from the tough Latin Kings boys. Almost everyone at the meeting stated that it was essential to separate Fernanda from the incipient gang influence. But after talking to her, Celia and Gordon formed another opinion: the more people told her not to mix with the Latin Kings, the more determined she was to continue, despite her admission that she didn't really like those boys that much; they were so macho and hostile and they did not really seem to like her, but merely tolerate her.

So Celia and Gordon took a different tack. They spoke to some of the other seemingly tough young male students in the school who were not connected with street gangs in any way and asked them what they did with their time. Some of them worked out at a nearby gym, where a former boxing pro who coached boxing would have nothing to do with drugs, gangs, or weapons. Fernanda took to the idea of getting training in boxing.

It doesn't, at face value, seem like an alternative to being aggressive, but it is a controlled environment in which there are physically demanding exercise routines (Fernanda said she had never seen a jump rope in her life before) which helped her slim down, feel better about herself, feel powerful, and able to impress peers. Celia joked that when she was a hairstylist she could give boxers at her gym a special discount, since all they would need was the number two clippers.

Restore

Gordon and Celia spent a lot of time talking to Fernanda about what she considered a fair consequence if she engaged in any of her aggressive, assaultive behavior against any other student in the school. She had quite a distorted idea of fairness, arguing that in every case someone else was the provocateur and initiated an insult of some kind. She did not feel any punishment was just, when all she was doing was exacting retribution. She argued that other girls were just as mean, but they used their cell phones to send hurtful messages and stir up trouble over boys.

There was a tiny grain of truth in these allegations, so in the end the decisions were not based on reason or on her acquiescing to a contingency. Under a directive from the dean of students, Gordon and Celia told Fernanda the hard truth: three strikes and you're out. Sorry, not our rule. The school requires it. If you retaliate or start a fight you will lose privileges. If you are being provoked or bullied you go straight to the dean. Stay out of conflict and you will be able to leave school at 16, keep going to the gym and get funding to go to the hairdressing academy, spend time with your *abuela* (grandma), and practice Spanish. It's your choice. Anything else your parents used to complain about, they now agree is entirely up to you—you can dress how you like, wear whatever jewelry you want, go out with any boy (he has to be a student at your school), keep your room as untidy as you want, sleep in on Saturdays—be a sloppy teenager if you want, just don't be a violent one. Fernanda liked this plan.

Think

Fernanda's apparent need to dominate others seemed to stem from many of her distorted social cognitions. Her learning disability made her feel inadequate in the areas where students around her were succeeding—academic work. Her lack of emotion competence (understanding her feelings and those of others around her) made her a poor judge of social and interpersonal relationships. She made inferences that other students were hostile and out to get her. She could not judge other people's feelings and had never experienced sufficient emotional closeness (attachment) to her hard-working parents to care much about their needs. She had achieved very few successes in her life; one area where she could feel superior was in physical domination. Constant parental criticism and trouble with school authorities made her feel worthless and ashamed. Knowing that other students did not like her, she went out of her way to prove she was unlikeable.

If she had not been aggressive, Fernanda's cognitive emotional pattern would almost certainly have earned her a mental health label—such as depressed, or maybe antisocial or borderline personality disorder. She certainly needed cognitive therapy to help her restructure many of these dysfunctional and negative ideas about herself and others. The psychologist at the mental health clinic, who originally had seen only her most negative side and had labeled her as psychopathic, agreed to offer 14 sessions of weekly cognitive-behavior therapy to address her cognitive distortions. It is beyond the scope of this teachers' guide to describe such psychotherapy in detail, but the basic idea is that the therapist uses a combination of metaphor, rational discourse, correction of misconceptions, anger management, thinking straight, and encouraging the client to test their assumptions. This is achieved by trying new behaviors, all designed to change her automatic thoughts and negative schemas about herself and others. There are a number of CBT programs designed for teenagers, which use humor, worksheets, and other practical materials—a good example freely available to qualified mental health professionals is Gary O'Reilly's *CBT Workbook for Children & Adolescents*. O'Reilly (Hayes & O'Reilly, 2007) has written about young people "on the cusp of criminality," which certainly describes Fernanda. He is a clinical psychologist at University College, Dublin, and apart from the Irish humor the materials are perfectly suitable for American teenagers!

Someone once said that in this world you have to be either smart or pleasant. Fernanda was not smart. It was a long road to make her pleasant. But she did leave school at 16 with no further reported incidents of violence at school and a Certificate of Completion. Her elderly boxing coach at the gym said she was an aggressive boxer but not a very good one—she would only improve when she learned to control her anger, which he thought would come in time. We do not know if Fernanda ever became a professional hairdresser, but she never became a member of the Latin Kings (or a Latin Queen as the females are called).

SUMMARY

In this chapter we introduced you to the four-component model and explained how each component needs to be addressed in any comprehensive intervention plan. The four components are based on simple assumptions: (1) inappropriate and negative behavior occurs in a context, so the key to prevention is to change those circumstances; (2) negative behavior serves a function—we need to teach more appropriate alternative skills that achieve similar motivational or emotional goals for the student; (3) consequences do matter but they must be restorative; they have to be appropriate, fair, and not likely to exacerbate the student's negative feelings; (4) a student's emotional needs and cognitive distortions need to be understood and addressed. A plan with these four components helps to generate hope and optimism, demonstrating to the most challenging students that they have lives of value. In the next chapter we pursue some of the practical requirements for implementing formal plans within a restorative ethos: school policies regarding discipline referral, restorative team meetings, in-school suspension, and crisis management.

8 Reflecting Schoolwide Policy in Teacher Practice

This chapter covers schoolwide systems and policies about behavioral issues reflected in teacher decisions and practice. Across the school, staff responses to behavior must be consistent, fair, and transparent to everyone to minimize the risk of arbitrary or overly punitive reactions and in order for restorative practices to proceed without misunderstandings and misinterpretations. The chapter covers strategies used to record discipline incidents that distinguish between major and minor behavior problems, including those that cause harm to others versus behaviors that need attention but are not a direct threat to the safety of any other person. Risk assessment for threats is addressed, along with description of a systematic process for the school to respond to threatening incidents. The chapter includes a discussion of how an objective description of incidents provides important information for future intervention planning as well as self-evaluation data.

MAKING DECISIONS ABOUT BEHAVIOR AND ITS CONSEQUENCES

It is important to make good judgments about the seriousness of behavioral incidents and to be able to estimate risk associated with different behaviors, what they signal, what the level of threat is, and how urgently behavior must be addressed. Seriousness does not dictate the type of punishment appropriate for behavior: this is characteristic of a system of retribution where "the punishment must fit the crime." In contrast, in a restorative discipline school, seriousness is focused on identifying the degree of harm (or potential for harm) and thus the level of restoration that is needed in order to redress that harm—to make amends or restitution, not just to punish.

Not all behaviors require school-based interventions: some instead suggest appropriate referrals for nonschool services or advice for the child and family. Teachers also need to be aware of behaviors that need attention even if they do not present a threat to others, such as self-harm behaviors (e.g., "cutting" and other forms of self-injury). Still other behaviors may put children at risk for the longer term, such as eating disorders that can contribute to behavioral difficulties. Obese children may be bullied and restrictive eating disorders such as anorexia and bulimia can have serious health consequences for adolescents. There are "victimless" behaviors such as being extremely isolated socially and students who have no friends may be at risk for becoming victims or even "aggressive victims" that could, in the future, cause harm to others. Certain inappropriate sexual behaviors do not directly harm other students but can become problematic and overt, such as accessing pornography beyond typical curiosity or voyeuristic behavior in the school's locker rooms and toilets. Finally, teachers must also be familiar with school discipline policies for behavior problems such as substance abuse that are not necessarily disruptive to school activities but interfere with successful learning.

In most schools when there is a critical incident, teachers have access to the consultant services of a capable behavior specialist such as a school psychologist or counselor to provide both ongoing advice and assistance. This consultant specialist has a designated role supporting restorative school discipline generally and also providing services as part of Level 1 and Level 2 interventions for eligible individual children (see the companion consultant's guide). A consultant with specialist knowledge has the expertise to help schools and teachers develop clear guidelines for how to respond to different behaviors.

Teachers must respond effectively to behaviors that are or have the potential to be harmful to other students. Judgments about behavior and how to react should not be left to the moment, as these kinds of reactions are highly likely to appear arbitrary to students. What can look like the very same behavior by two different children (e.g., talking back to the teacher in class when reprimanded) should not lead to different consequences that can in turn appear to be unfair. Lack of transparency about discipline decisions results in mistrust and suspicion regarding equity and discrimination. Particularly for children who have ongoing behavioral challenges, lack of transparency as to how the school responds to incidents reinforces negative attributions that the entire system is hostile. Interpretations of unfairness and discrimination are logical conclusions for children (and families) who feel they are always treated differently and unfairly in comparison to others who are favored or seen as having more power in the school community. Given that these are likely to be the students who most often are engaged in behavioral incidents, teachers need to be careful that they are not providing justification for negative feelings for children who consider that they are once again being treated unfairly. Breaking this cycle is particularly important to build trust that supports new, positive behaviors and inclusion.

How does the teacher judge the seriousness of an offense? There are some simple principles that can be applied. For example in a case of assault, what sort of weapons if any were used, what sorts of threats were made, was the violence triggered by anger or by fear, has the behavior occurred before? In the analysis of criminal behavior, understanding what is called the "offense chain" is important—what sequence of events led up to the behavior, was it planned or opportunistic? It is also important when interviewing young people who have committed a serious transgression to allow the interview to elicit the kinds of possibly distorted thinking that preceded an aggressive incident. Good interview techniques by the teacher who records and reports an incident can provide helpful information about whether the child is remorseful, the degree to which he or she understands the seriousness of the offense, and whether he or she has empathy for the victim. Young people with psychopathic traits need to be managed very differently from those who made a silly mistake and genuinely regret it. Note, too, that while restorative practices are underway, there may also be natural consequences for some behavior such as aggression and criminal offenses. Even when the offense is punished (retribution), the punishment doesn't replace the need for restoration (making things right again) and working toward ensuring no future repetitions of the behavior. These issues are closely related to the likelihood of success with a restorative practices approach.

Schools with restorative practices have in place fair and transparent rules for student conduct along with stated consequences for behavior outside the rules. The principal has adopted a restorative practices ethos as the foundation for behavior expectations that are both understood and considered to be fair across the school community (Chapter 1). Other schoolwide approaches to challenging behavior such as Schoolwide Positive Behavior Support (SWPBS) also require that schools specify objective, observable definitions of expectations for student behavior along with transparency about the kinds of consequences, based on the nature and extent of particular behaviors (Sugai et al., 2005). If positive approaches to school discipline are to work, they must build on shared understandings about school behavioral expectations along with a set of processes and recording procedures to monitor student behavior and what happens as a result of that behavior. This goes beyond stating positive examples of a school's behavioral expectations (Chapter 2) to require careful delineation of acceptable and unacceptable behavior, along with decisions about whether an unacceptable behavior is minor or major.

RECORDING BEHAVIORAL INCIDENTS OBJECTIVELY

Several statistics provide evidence regarding behavioral challenges for schools. One such metric is the number and percentage of Office Discipline Referrals (ODRs) filed by school personnel to record serious student behavior, which may or may not result in students being sent to the office but does result in a report or record of the incident (McIntosh, Campbell, Carter, & Zumbo, 2009). Some school systems also require and utilize formal student threat assessment reports that must be filed with the district (Strong & Cornell, 2008). These reporting devices may already be required by the school district but not necessarily used at the school as part of an ongoing process of restorative practices. A well-functioning mechanism for office referrals fulfills district reporting requirements and also provides the teacher and others at the school with information useful for intervention planning.

Office Discipline Referral (ODR)

A system of Office Discipline Referrals (ODR) is a formal process for recording, compiling, and analyzing incidents when student behavior fails to meet the behavior expectations established for the school. Virtually all schools have such a system in place. Every teacher should know when and how to complete an ODR according to school policy. A good ODR simultaneously serves several purposes:

- Sufficient detail about incidents of problem behavior are reported using agreed definitions across the school, which are transparent to and understood by students, school personnel, and families
- The requirement to file a formal incident record for minor and major behavior problems helps to protect teachers and students from charges of arbitrary application of discipline rules and consequences

- The accumulation of ODRs for a particular individual child should signal the need for advice to break negative interaction patterns as well as getting additional services and supports
- Regular monitoring of ODRs allows identification of particular classrooms where staff may require additional specialist support or professional development to manage student behavior
- If the ODRs occur most often for students who share a particular demographic, reflect on the possibility that subtle discrimination, racism, or personal feelings of dislike towards particular children is affecting a teacher's judgment or making specific children feel ignored or rejected (e.g., disproportionate referrals for students from a particular ethnic group compared with those who are regarded as part of the dominant culture)
- Analyses of ODRs at the grade level, in different school contexts, and across subjects and types of learning activities can help identify particular challenges (e.g., frequent discipline reports in school hallways and walkways suggests the need for problem solving that might remedy "unsafe" environments for students)
- Team problem solving using examples of particular types of problem behaviors could lead to the design of schoolwide interventions to address particular issues that appear to be endemic (e.g., incidents of fighting, inappropriate physical contact, assault, abusive language, teasing, and harassment may reveal patterns of bullying requiring systematic attention)
- Ongoing evaluation of the ODRs enables assessment of the extent to which restorative practices are effective and meeting both the teacher's and the students' needs

Every teacher must be familiar with the school's formal process for recording behavioral incidents and referrals to the office. In addition, examining your own referrals for any troubling patterns, either regarding your own practices or your children's behaviors, is enormously helpful in maintaining a positive classroom environment.

What to Include in Incident Reports for ODRs

Once clear behavior expectations for your school and classroom are stated, violations of those expectations and consequences can be defined and agreed. Just as it was important to reach agreement across the school regarding behavior expectations, there must be agreement across the school about behaviors that do not meet those expectations. This too is a process that requires discussion and negotiation across the school so that teachers can deal with children fairly and consistently and so that children (and their families) perceive that treatment is fair and consistent.

Table 6 provides an exemplary *Incident Report for Office Discipline Referrals* that is the result of an extensive consultation process across a school following detailed consideration to reach consensus about what problem behaviors would be targeted.

Table 6   Incident Report for Office Discipline Referrals

Incident Report for Office Discipline Referrals (ODRs)							
Name:		Grade in school:			Referring staff:		
Date:		Time of incident:					
(one ✓) **Location:**							
Classroom		Restrooms		Admin		Buses	
Outside areas		Library		Staffroom		School trips	
Hall/ walkways		Sports facilities		Auditorium			
Stairwell		School frontage/ community		Cafeteria		Other	

(one ✓) **Minor Problem Behavior**		(one ✓) **Major Problem Behavior**		(one ✓) **Actions Taken**	
Inappropriate language		Abusive language/ profanity		Dialogue/conference with student/class	
Inappropriate physical contact		Fighting/physical aggression		Reprimand	
Defiance, disrespect (phone, walkman, water bombs)		Defiance/disrespect		Parent contact	
Disruption to class		Disruption to class		Student makes amends	
Lying/cheating		Lying/cheating		Related consequences	
Teasing		Harassment/tease/ taunt		Detention	
Property misuse/damage		Lateness (at least 3x)		Demerit	
(one ✓) **Possible Motivation**		Forgery/ theft		In-school suspension	
Obtain peer attention		Skipping class/ truancy			
Obtain adult attention		Property misuse/ damage			

	Obtain item/activities		Substance abuse (drugs, alcohol)		**Resolved by**	
	Avoid tasks/activities		Arson		Referring staff	
	Avoid peer/s		Weapons		Homeroom teacher	
	Avoid adult		Bomb/fireworks		Head of Department Dean	
	Don't know					
(one ✓) **Others involved**					**(Sign)**	
	None		Teacher aide		**OR**	
	Peer/s		Substitute teacher		Refer to Senior Management Team (see below)	
	Staff		Other_____ (list)			
Other information:						
1.						
2.						
3.						
	Action by Senior Management Team		Asst. Principal		Principal	
			Deputy Principal		Computer entry	

Source: Adapted with permission from SWIS Referral Form Examples in Todd, Horner, and Dickey (2010).

This system should differentiate between "major" and "minor" transgressions, and teachers should agree which behaviors fall into the two categories to prevent misunderstandings and inconsistencies that reinforce students' feelings of unfairness and even discrimination. An incident meeting the definition of either a "minor problem behavior" or a "major problem behavior" requires teachers to complete the descriptive portion of the Incident Report and submit it to the school office, even if the incident is managed within the classroom. Basic identifying information, including the child's name, year level, date, time of incident, and the referring staff member are entered along with the location where the incident occurred. The Incident Report is completed by the designated office manager (e.g., the deputy principal who carries schoolwide responsibility for reporting on disciplinary issues) based on information supplied by the referring teacher, the student, and others.

A crucial component of the record is identification of the transgression as a "minor problem behavior" or a "major problem behavior" according to agreed definitions that are provided as part of the process. These definitions may be school specific but they must be transparent to staff, students, and families. The important principle is that the definitions are agreed across the school to ensure disciplinary consistency and fairness. Because some behaviors can be considered to be either minor or major problems (e.g., "disruption to class"), the definitions must sort these two groups as objectively as possible. Teasing, for example, may be a minor problem behavior if there appeared to be no intent to hurt, but teasing is a major problem behavior if the behaviors escalate, show intent to hurt, and/or evidence racism, sexism, or other forms of prejudice.

Table 7 provides some examples of minor and major problem behaviors consistent with the sample *Incident Report for ODRs* in Table 6.

Table 7   Minor versus Major Behavior Problems in Schools

Minor Problem Behavior	Major Problem Behavior
Inappropriate language	Abusive language/swearing at others
Inappropriate physical contact	Fighting, assault
Defiance, disrespect (e.g., delayed response)	Defiance, disrespect (e.g., refusals)
Disruption to class (e.g., talking to another student)	Disruption to class (repeatedly talking out of turn)
Lying/cheating (e.g., asking someone for an answer to a question)	Lying/cheating (e.g., cheating on a final exam, changing one's grade, plagiarism)
Teasing (e.g., a humorous remark that does not appear to have hostile intent)	Teasing/harassment (e.g., behaviors unacceptable to recipient, including text bullying, racist remarks, name calling)
Lateness (a few minutes late on more than one occasion)	Lateness (persistent and lengthy lateness without a valid reason)
Property misuse/damage (unintentional breakage through using equipment in an inappropriate area or at inappropriate time)	Property misuse/damage (intentional damage of any kind, including graffiti, and particularly if item/s are expensive)
n/a	Forgery/theft
n/a	Substance abuse (alcohol, drugs, including failure to report drug possession or supplying at school; possession of drug paraphernalia)
n/a	Weapons (possession of offensive weapon, including knife, gun, needles or other object with intent to injure others)
n/a	Bomb threat (including trying to make a bomb)
n/a	Arson (setting fires, possessing lighter or matches in school)

Our sample incident report includes additional information about possible motivations for the behavior, who else was involved, and space for additional information that might be relevant to understanding what happened. The report also includes a log of the outcome (the behavior consequence for the student), actions taken by the school's senior management team, and initialing by the person completing the report. This too is important, as analyses over time might reveal that, regardless of actions taken, previous consequences delivered to particular students appear to be having no effect and behaviors continue to reoccur. These examples have been adapted (modified by using descriptors commonly used in the United States) from those developed for a secondary school in a small town in New Zealand implementing Schoolwide Positive Behavior Support. The process was seen as relevant to New Zealand needs and found to be helpful for the schools that used it (Savage et al., 2011).

RESTORATIVE CONFERENCING AT SCHOOL LEVEL

All teachers have major responsibility to ensure that restorative practices are well established at the classroom level and throughout the school, including teacher-supervised places outside the classroom. While the less formal and ongoing restorative practices are the teacher's responsibility, there will be occasions when serious behavior requires that a restorative conference be convened by the principal at the school level. A restorative conference is a formal meeting of those who are directly involved in a particular incident in which harm has been caused or perceived as being imminent. Those included in the conference are the student(s) who is (are) the "offender(s)," those who are the "victims," a trained facilitator (e.g., the principal, dean, or school psychologist), and the teachers, peers, family members, and others who are concerned parties.

When Is a Restorative Conference Needed?

The need for a formal restorative conference is signaled by the nature of the incident and serious behavior that may result in consequences for the offender such as an in-school suspension, but the important point is that the conference is crucial and any consequences do not replace the need for restoration conferencing. Teachers and other school personnel develop shared understandings about the kinds of incidents and behaviors that require a school-level response such as a formal restorative conference, and these are obviously initiated through the Office Discipline Referral process. Restorative conferences may also be held as responses to challenging schoolwide issues, such as bullying that may have become widespread in the school restrooms, corridors, and other school environments outside the classroom. Teachers are most likely to be involved in restorative conferences that are focused on a particular student for whom a Level 2 or Level 3 intervention is being planned following a series of actions that do not seem to be working for that student.

What Should Be the Goal of a Restorative Conference?

The major purpose of the conference is to achieve consensus about the nature of the problem and gather ideas about what actions can be taken for making amends in a way that allows participants to move forward in a positive way. The conference process addresses each of the following issues:

- Providing the victims with a voice and meeting the needs of victims
- Ensuring that the views of all those who are involved in an incident are heard and respected
- Establishing a process that builds on a restorative ethos—consequences may follow particular behaviors, but these are part of a restorative process not used as punishment but as an end goal in itself

The restorative conference is not about blaming, nor is it about forgiveness or denying harm that may have occurred. Rather, the challenge is to keep the conversation respectful of the dignity of everyone involved. Without great care, a group meeting can quickly become a kind of public retribution in which group participants may gang up on an offender or even a victim so that the activity adds to harm. Hence, the meeting is facilitated by either the school principal or school psychologist who follows careful guidelines for restoration rather than retribution.

Who Should Facilitate the Restorative Conference?

A restorative conference can be facilitated successfully by a school psychologist, deputy principal, dean, or a respected member of the community. In small schools, it may be desirable for the principal to serve as facilitator for some or even all restorative conferences. Criteria for who can serve as the facilitator include identifying someone who (a) is not directly involved in an "incident" so is more likely to be seen as a neutral party; (b) has the authority within the school and community to invite relevant parties and to follow through to ensure that plans that are developed are implemented and evaluated; and (c) has undertaken the required study and practice in restorative conferencing for effective facilitation according to restorative practices. Ideally, the school has a minimum of two trained facilitators who are committed to the process, one of whom might be external to the school (e.g., a community support person) but available on contract when needed. (Details regarding training of restorative conference facilitators are included in the consultant's guide.)

Administrative Support for Restorative Conferences

An important reason why the principal assumes special responsibility for the conduct of restorative conferences is that various provisions must be made. There are scheduling considerations, including school staff, family, and student time commitments: a restorative conference may require release time for school personnel or either payment or time *in lieu* (compensatory time) for conferences held outside normal school hours. Arrangements need to be made to ensure safe transportation for all participants, and some funds may be needed to provide food and drink at the start of the conference. If a community support person is identified who is trained and can be "on call" for restorative conferencing, this service can be budgeted at an hourly rate and the school might budget on the basis that there will be between five to ten such conferences in a typical school year. Fewer than this number suggests that a school is not taking on restorative practices at a school level, and a higher number—especially at smaller schools—may indicate that incidents are being allowed to escalate in classrooms throughout the school rather than being addressed through restorative practices. In addition, schoolwide use of restorative conferencing should be integrated within the regional or districtwide services available to individual schools through specialist behavioral support or a school psychologist. Even when a specially trained facilitator is used for a school's restorative conferencing rather than the school psychologist performing this role, the school's behavioral specialist should be kept informed and even directly involved in particular conferences. For example, the school psychologist's support is especially helpful in planning a schoolwide response to bullying and also for planning focused on a specific child whose behavior has not responded to systems already in place at the school. The next chapter addresses this issue in more detail where services to individual children are part of the planning.

IN-SCHOOL SUSPENSION

In any school, suspending a student is a serious issue, and increases in suspensions overall are of concern to everyone. Young people are suspended for behaviors that challenge adults and their schools, and many of these youth also exhibit learning difficulties. When dealing with severe behaviors, failure to intervene effectively and early can lead to the development of ongoing conduct disorders that become increasingly intractable as the child grows older. Suspension is generally seen as a last resort response that can protect others in the environment from the child's behavior and also communicate a clear message to the child and his family that some behavior cannot be tolerated in classrooms and in the school. Nevertheless, there are serious problems with disciplinary exclusion that entails removal of children from school altogether, whether this is for a brief period or, as sometimes happens, permanently. Also, an issue that continues to challenge communities is the ongoing evidence—as recently as a large-scale investigation published in 2011—that children of color are disproportionately overrepresented in school exclusion statistics (Vincent & Tobin, 2011).

Suspension does provide temporary "relief" for schools as well as behavioral consequences for the children involved. Suspension can also remove the risk of harm to other students and to the teacher. However, there are other risks that suspension can create:

- Students sent home from school miss valuable learning opportunities and fall further behind academically
- Students may be unsupervised or poorly supervised once they leave school, creating the potential for further behavioral difficulties to develop
- Particularly for teenagers, the suspended student may actually encourage peers to be truant to join them while away from school
- Sending students away from school may actually function as a "reward" for some children and youth; it also allows escape from aversive classroom and academic experiences—resulting in negative reinforcement
- Where there are obvious racial and cultural differences evident in disproportionate suspensions of students from some groups in comparison to others, a message of unfairness or even racism can subtly (or not so subtly) be the main message communicated to students throughout the school
- When students are excluded from school, for any reason, this can function as a negative message that—whenever the going gets tough—they are in fact not wanted and do not belong in the school community. (A metaphor for this would be parents having their child removed from the family based on bad behavior—just as this shouldn't be a consequence at home, it cannot be a consequence at school)

- Families may lack the capacity to provide a structured and constructive environment for them while out of school, hence following suspension they may return to school with even more problems

A restorative approach to serious behavior allows the student to make amends, works to repair damage, and maintains the school's major purpose to be educative in ensuring that the student in suspension does not fall further behind academically while suspended. In-school suspension for severe behavior shifts the purpose of suspension from punishment to natural consequences that clearly communicate behavior is unacceptable in a manner that doesn't introduce further risks but is instead restorative and maintains high expectations for the student.

Key principles for in-school suspension consistent with an overall restorative school discipline framework are:

- The student remains a valued member of his or her school community, even while serious consequences are being delivered for unacceptable behavior
- The student continues to be responsible for his or her learning, and negative behavior does not provide a pathway to avoid school work and completion of curriculum requirements
- The student participates in constructive, educative processes towards reshaping more positive behavior as well as continuing to learn throughout disciplinary procedures
- Both adults and the student engage in a process of restoration and mutual understanding rather than a process of blame and punishment
- The school maintains its commitment to every student's full participation in the school community and the learning opportunities it offers
- Consequences for behavior are not delivered at the expense of learning and opportunity for positive behavior change

For in-school suspension to work, it must be one component of a schoolwide comprehensive approach to restorative school discipline. It is not a substitute for an overall commitment to Restorative Classroom Discipline (Chapter 1); schoolwide and classroom behavioral expectations (Chapter 2); culturally responsive relationships with families and the community (Chapter 3); classroom climates and culturally responsive pedagogies where children feel membership (Chapter 4); classroom and peer support structures (Chapter 5); individualized child-focused intervention services (Chapter 6 and 7); fair and transparent schoolwide responses to behavioral challenges and incidents (Chapter 8); data system for team planning and monitoring progress (Chapter 9); and professional development (Chapter 10). Traditional approaches to children whose relationships have been damaged or broken because of their behavior in an incident causing harm has been to exclude them—with an out-of-school suspension or exclusion consequence operating outside the educational purposes of school—and communicating powerful messages about punitive resolution of conflict. Instead, this chapter builds on a metaphorical loop whereby actions taken to resolve conflict must cycle back to the principles and values of peaceful resolution of conflict. Actions taken following conflict must allow participants to be heard, must allow amends to be made, and must not jeopardize any child's safety or educational future. Thus, the process of in-school suspension presented here closes the loop so that schoolwide restorative practices are reflected at all levels of prevention and intervention, including how the school responds to the most serious behavior.

It is crucial that in-school suspension functions exactly parallel to how out-of-school suspension previously was used. That is, use of in-school suspension is the consequence for serious behavior incidents (according to processes specified in the school's discipline policy) and cannot be accessed more frequently or for "lesser" behavior *simply because the room is there* to avoid addressing behavior management challenges in the classroom. Nor should it be seen as a next-to-final resort where the school uses a standard suspension hanging as a threat over the heads of adults and children whenever in-school suspension is judged to have "not worked."

The message must be clear and unambiguous: Nothing a child does will result in exclusion from school and/or excusing a student from his or her learning responsibilities. Remember too that in-school suspension *replaces* out-of-school suspension—it is not another level of punishment! From a restorative practices perspective, the only circumstances that can justify removing the child from the school building are (a) a threat assessment identifying that the child has made a serious substantive threat of violence (discussed later in this chapter) and/or (b) that the child is arrested or detained for a crime.

Key Components of In-School Suspension

At least the following components should be included in an in-school suspension system:

- *Shared Understandings and Knowledge:* All staff practices must be consistent with the school's behavior expectations, schoolwide discipline policy and restorative practices, individualized supports for students, and team and network supports for staff.

- *Professional Development:* Teachers should have access to professional development on Restorative Classroom Discipline, and earlier in this guide we describe some of the crucial skills needed for restorative practices. Part of this training should cover policy and practices for in-school suspension, including the responsibilities of the referring classroom teacher who also should be asked to participate in communications describing the rationale and procedures for in-school suspension to families and members of the community.

- *The In-School Suspension Schedule:* The teacher plays an important role in supporting students who are under an in-school suspension. On any given day, each student's full-day schedule will not align with the general schedule for bathroom breaks, recess, and lunch periods so that there will be no time overlap between suspended students' times out of the room and those of other students at the school, particularly for students in the same age or grade range as those suspended. However, it is the subject teacher (secondary) or grade-level teacher (elementary) who will assist the in-school suspension supervisor work out an appropriate schedule for the student.

- *The Teacher-Student Contract:* For any of the students who are assigned to in-school suspension, there is a teacher-student in-school suspension contract. This contract needs to include the student's daily requirements aligned with curriculum activities during suspension, including homework and any assessments or assignments expected of classmates who are not suspended during that same timeframe.

- *Home-School Communications:* As the teacher, you'll also assist in establishing an individually appropriate home-school communication protocol for daily reporting from school to home and from home to school regarding activities in the in-school suspension room and follow through requirements for home (generally this is expected homework). We have included a model *Home-School, In-School Suspension Contract* to make these communications transparent (see Table 8).

- *Ongoing Monitoring and Support:* Both the student and the teacher complete the *In-School Suspension Reflections.* Sample reflection sheets are provided in Table 9. Following the guidelines developed for the student's daily schoolwork assignments, you as the teacher provide regular feedback (at least every 2 days) to the student on work. You are also part of the restorative conference process for returning the child to the classroom at the end of the suspension period.

Table 8 The Home-School, In-School Suspension Contract

The Home-School, In-School Suspension Contract

Description of the Incident Leading to In-School Suspension:

Date/time of the Restorative School Conference:

Location of the Conference:

Who From the Family (and Relationship) Will Be Attending:

Contract

The principal or his/her representative has discussed with me the incident resulting in in-school suspension and procedures required for restoration and restitution. I understand that my son/daughter will be required to keep up to date with his/her schoolwork during the time spent in in-school suspension, and I agree to support him/her in this process, including supervision of homework. Further, I agree to participate in regular communication as described below with both the staff supervisor of the in-school suspension room and the teacher who is named below. My son/daughter has also signed below to indicate his/her acceptance of these terms.

Parent Signature: Date:

Student Signature: Date:

Staff Supervisor Signature: Date:

Classroom Teacher Signature: Date:

Principal Signature: Date:

Communication process (describe briefly):

Table 9   Forms for In-School Suspension Reflections

In-School Suspension Reflections

Student Reflection   Name: _____

Teacher/staff name: _____

The purpose behind this sheet is to help you reflect on what happened, why, and what the next steps are from here. It is not about blame and punishment, but is about working things out for the better. This sheet will be seen by the teacher and the consultant.

Please answer the questions honestly and clearly.

1. Do you think it was fair that you were sent to in-school suspension? Why?

2. What were you doing when you were sent?

3. What were you thinking or feeling when you were sent?

4. Did your behavior affect other students? How?

5. What could you have done differently so that you could stay in class?

6. What things need to change for you to return to class?

Please leave this with the in-school suspension teacher.

(Continued)

Table 9 (Continued)

Staff In-School Suspension Reflection   Name: _____

Student name: _____

The purpose behind this sheet is to reflect on what happened, why and what the next steps are from here. It is not about blame and punishment, but is about working things out for the better. The student has a similar sheet to complete.

7. What was the student's behavior that resulted in being sent to in-school suspension?

8. What prior interventions were done before sending the student to in-school suspension?

9. Were other students affected by the behavior, who was affected, and how?

10. What could you have done differently that may have resulted in the student modifying his/her behavior?

11. How can you change classroom practices in the future to manage this student's behavior?

12. What happens next with this student?

Please keep this sheet, as it will be useful as part of the working-through process. You may wish to discuss it with the Principal, Dean, or Head of Department.

These forms are adapted from procedures used at a New Zealand high school, Paeroa College, 2008.

SUICIDE PREVENTION, INTERVENTION, AND POSTVENTION

Suicide is a leading cause of death for young people aged 10 to 24 in the United States, according to the most recent figures available from the Centers for Disease Control and Prevention (2010). In their survey of members of the National Association of School Psychologists (NASP), Nickerson and Zhe (2004) reported that suicide attempts (along with student-to-student assault and a student's serious illness or accidental death) were among the most frequent crisis events in which school psychologists were involved as part of school crisis response teams. And while most suicides involve individual children and youth, it is also worth remembering that young people responsible for high-profile school shootings have also been suicidal. Clearly, the school psychologist and the principal have particular responsibilities for evaluating risk, recommending actions, making appropriate referrals, and supporting school, student, and family in suicide prevention and intervention. But teachers play a crucial role in identifying risk, establishing classroom interactions that support students rather than inadvertently creating the conditions for student victimization, and assisting in debriefing student suicide in the context of small groups and nurturing classroom environments. Teachers need to be well prepared for their part on the school team so that for the child who may be suicidal, other staff in the room, classmates, and students' families receive the appropriate advice and support when there is a suicide threat or crisis.

Suicide is rare below the age of 10, but it does occur so that even elementary school teachers need to develop skills in suicide prevention and intervention. Given the increased risk during adolescence, however, the issue has particular relevance for middle and high school teachers. Prevention and intervention programs generally emphasize information for teachers about risk factors and warning signs for suicide; basic information for students about recognizing risk, how to respond to a peer, and whom to tell; and appropriate procedures and resource personnel to respond to suicide ideation and threats in school, including involvement of the family. The whole-school response after a completed suicide—termed *postvention* by the American Association of Suicidology—is also important given concerns about suicide contagion and copycat suicide.

Responding to Risk for Student Suicide

A great deal is known empirically about risk factors for suicide. There are demographic and personal characteristics associated with higher rates of suicide. Suicide is the second leading cause of death among Native American/Alaska Native youth, and white males have the highest completed suicide rates. Hispanic, African American, and gay, lesbian, and bisexual youth have high rates of attempted suicides, and girls are more likely than boys to attempt suicide (Centers for Disease Control and Prevention, 2010; D'Augelli et al., 2005). One-third to one-half of students attempting suicide has depression, and those at risk for suicide exhibit other symptoms such as pessimism and hopelessness. School-related symptoms include truancy, suspensions, school dropout rates before graduation, low achievement, school alienation, and lack of engagement (Fergusson, Beautrais, & Horwood, 2003). Precipitating events are known to be the loss of someone close (through death or breakup of a relationship, e.g., with a boyfriend); contagion; being victimized or rejected by peers; failing to achieve valued goals (e.g., low test scores; being rejected for study at a top university after graduation); confusion about sexual identity; and a recent disciplinary event that was humiliating for the student (American Psychological Association, 2004).

Debski et al. (2007) report key behavioral warning signs of a potentially suicidal student:

- Increase in drug or alcohol use
- Communicating thoughts of suicide
- Preoccupation with death
- Giving away prized possessions
- Making final arrangements and saying good-bye
- Increased moodiness, withdrawal, or acting out
- Major changes in eating or sleeping habits
- Expressions of hopelessness, guilt, or worthlessness, or intense anger towards oneself or others
- Drop in school performance
- Loss of interest in usual activities
- Having a plan for suicide (p. 159)

Debski et al. (2007) emphasize that whenever a teacher observes a number of these signs in a student, parental consent is not required for an initial interview with the student as part of assessing for suicide risk. The teacher should discuss concerns with a trained mental health professional at the school, such as the school psychologist, who would generally conduct the interview and carry out the necessary follow-through, including contact with the family.

If a student shows signs of serious risk for suicide, the school psychologist expects the parents to come to school for a conference, they are advised to keep a careful watch over their child, to remove access to any means of self-harm (e.g., any guns), and to seek professional mental health advice from someone with expertise on suicide. When an attempt has been made or threatened, the student should be held under close supervision and watched carefully until the parents can pick him or her up—and *never* be sent home alone. If the family seems unwilling to follow up to keep the child safe, Brock and Sandoval (1997) advise that they be warned that failure to seek assistance is neglectful and the school will contact child protective services.

What to Do in the Classroom

Teachers are often in the best position to hear from peers that a student is contemplating suicide. Teenagers do talk about suicide with their friends, but Juhnke, Granello, and Granello (2011) report that only about a quarter of students will tell an adult that their friend is considering suicide. Based on their extensive practitioner and research experience, these authors stress that teachers need to communicate to their students the importance of not keeping such secrets but sharing the information with a trusted adult. In addition to recognizing risk and alerting the school principal, teachers can communicate adaptive reactions to suicide threat and completion. Note too that the increased risk of suicide for certain student groups (students from minority cultural groups, who are gay or lesbian, etc.) also emphasizes how important it is that teachers establish a warm classroom climate where individual students are not bullied or victimized but feel they belong and have support from their peers and friends.

According to the experts, talking about suicide is not only okay but can actually reduce risk. However, this discussion needs to communicate the right messages rather than create a context that can sensationalize or glorify suicide. School personnel sometimes communicate the unfortunate message that a student has committed suicide in an attempt to "end the pain." School personnel need to communicate clearly that suicide does not end pain, but rather passes it on to friends, family, and the whole community— who now must live with guilt and lifelong regret. There is some evidence of suicide contagion or copycat suicides that can occur following a first suicide. Contagion suicide is most likely to occur among close peers, and experts associate copycat suicides with activities that seem to glamorize or dramatize the suicide. Teachers and other school personnel want to show that they care, but holding in-school memorials, candle vigils, and creating shrines with pictures, flowers, and teddy bears can make suicide appear to be a glamorous death and a way for other lonely young people to seek what appears to be adoration. As an example, consider what happens in the aftermath of the death of a celebrity—particularly a rock star. Under ambiguous circumstances thought to be suicide, the consequence has enhanced the star's fame in death far beyond his or her reputation in life.

After a suicide attempt or a completed suicide, there are a number of appropriate procedures to follow so that other students at the school have appropriate support and to prevent the possibility of any other suicides in the future. Schools need to plan in advance and have a crisis team in place—trained for any crisis, not just suicide—rather than being reactive and thus unprepared. The American Association of Suicidology (1998) and others recommend the following school response to attempted and completed suicides:

- Verify the suicide report, keep the student safe, and contact the family, telling them of the school's intervention efforts and offer of assistance.
- Notify other students in the school by providing accurate information, being careful not to glamorize or dramatize the suicide situation.
- Notification to the other students should not be through an announcement over the public address system or in an assembly, but rather in one of two ways: (a) if homeroom teachers are knowledgeable and sufficiently well-briefed to handle this, have homeroom teachers tell the students what has happened during the same school period; or (b) have an experienced, trained staff member (this could be the school psychologist or a dean) follow the student's schedule through the day and talk individually with each class group.
- When sharing the information with students, reassure students that the student who attempted suicide is receiving help but keep details about the attempt confidential. Encourage students to discuss how to support one another, to express their feelings, and acknowledge feelings of responsibility or guilt but emphasize that no one could predict the suicide. Talk about resources for students to get further help, if needed.
- All teachers and other school staff, administrators, and the school's crisis response team who dealt with the incident must also document all actions taken according to district and school requirements.

Experts advise strongly against cancelling school for the day or helping to organize student attendance at the funeral of a student who has completed suicide (and use the phrase "completed suicide" not *successful* suicide: why?). If possible, the parents could be encouraged to have the funeral outside of school hours so that those who wish to attend can. If it is held within school hours, the principal should not provide transportation or cancel classes but should allow those students to attend who wish to do so (Poland & McCormick, 1999).

Immediately after an attempted or completed suicide, teachers need to be on the alert for signs of suicide contagion or, alternatively, guilt feelings. Additional support should be provided to those closest to the student.

Again, virtually all experts and clinicians working in the area of suicide agree that it is important to communicate to others that suicide is not a good solution to problems. It is also important to be careful not to demean the suicide victim in any way (Brock, 2002).

Teacher Self-Assessment

Table 10 lists true and false statements about suicide prevention and intervention based on available empirical evidence as reported by Debski et al. (2007). Every teacher should be familiar with the correct answers to each statement on the list. School policy and procedures as well as individual teacher practices should be consistent with the evidence on what we know about suicide rather than being based on what someone thinks or believes is true. We have produced the list with a true/false response column for use by teachers to test their knowledge on the inventory (correct answers are provided in the last column).

Table 10 Test Your Knowledge About What to Do for Suicide-Related Incidents

Statement About Suicide	Circle T for True or F for False	Correct Answer
Prevention actions consistent with the literature:		
1 Class discussions and literature on teen suicide should be avoided in schools because they may be triggers to suicidal behavior.	T F	False
2 The more detailed the suicide plan, the greater the likelihood the adolescent will complete a suicide.	T F	True
3 If a student is a minor and at risk for suicide but parents refuse to seek treatment, it is appropriate to warn them that child protective services may be called.	T F	True
4 When it is suspected a student may be suicidal, it is ethically permissible for the psychologist to conduct a risk assessment without first obtaining parental consent.	T F	True
5 The best predictor of a future suicide attempt is a past attempt.	T F	True
6 Research has shown that psychologists can predict suicide attempts with a high degree of accuracy.	T F	False
7 It is never permissible to ask about students' private thoughts and plans without first discussing the boundaries of confidentiality, even if a student may be suicidal.	T F	False

(Continued)

Table 10 (Continued)

Statement About Suicide	Circle T for True or F for False	Correct Answer
Postvention actions consistent with the literature:		
8 The school should identify the death as "accidental" and avoid mention of "suicide" so as to prevent suicide contagion.	T F	False
9 Postvention should begin immediately after the tragedy.	T F	True
10 The school should notify all students of the death by announcement on the public address system.	T F	False
11 The school should verify the facts and treat the death as a suicide.	T F	True
12 The school should provide busing, during school hours, for students who wish to attend funeral services, when consent is given by parents.	T F	False
13 The school should not glorify the death and not allow memorials dedicated to the school victim.	T F	True
What to do/say to a student who is close to another student who has committed suicide:		
14 Encourage the student to take control of his/her feelings so as not to get too emotional at school.	T F	False
15 Tell the student that the other student made a foolish decision because he/she was selfish and immature.	T F	False
16 Assure the student that his/her feelings of guilt, anger, grief, and confusion are normal.	T F	True
27 Assure the student that the other student is the only one responsible for his/her actions.	T F	True
18 Assure the student that no one could have foreseen the other student's suicide.	T F	True
19 Remind the student that suicide is a poor choice to solve problems.	T F	True
General school postvention actions consistent with the literature:		
20 When interviewed by the media after a student suicide at school, psychologists should disclose what they know about the deceased student and his or her family because the public has a right to know.	T F	False
21 Research suggests that suicide clusters or suicide contagion is a myth.	T F	False
22 After a student suicide, it is better for schools to refer students to a community agency for grief counseling rather than to provide it at school.	T F	False

THREAT ASSESSMENT

Sometimes the statements made by students (or adults) in schools may go beyond "ordinary" verbal aggression or harassment (whether minor or major), such as threats of future violence that are alarming and frightening. The occurrence of tragedies such as the shootings at Columbine High School in Colorado in 1999, at Red Lake High School in Minnesota in 2005, at the Amish school in Pennsylvania in 2006, and at Virginia Tech University in 2007 emphasize the role of *threat assessment* in preventing violence in schools, where there are large concentrations of children and adults who can be at risk. Threat assessment was originally developed by the U.S. Secret Service to identify risk to public officials from verbal and/ or written threats to commit a violent act against prominent figures and others (Strong & Cornell, 2008).

Threat assessment is different from "profiling" that labels characteristics of people likely to commit violence, hence it would be inappropriate to decide that a particular student has characteristics that make him or her dangerous to others without additional evidence of intent to harm. Threat assessment is *in response to a person's specific threatening behavior.* In addition, threat assessment requires a judgment about whether the person who has made a threat *is actually likely to carry out the threat.*

Teachers are familiar with what are sometimes called "empty" threats, shouted in the heat of the moment. Threats such as "I'll teach him a lesson" or "You'll get yours" are verbal behaviors that are socially unacceptable and generally lead to consequences as well as hard feelings and even fear. But some threats using the very same words may actually foreshadow violence and harm that could have been prevented had those words been taken seriously.

Cornell and Sheras (2006) have written a useful and practical set of *Guidelines for Responding to Student Threats of Violence* and provide a definition of a threat:

What Is a Threat?

*A threat is **an expression of intent to harm someone**. Threats may be spoken, written, or expressed in some way, such as through gestures. Threats may be direct ("I am going to beat you up") or indirect ("I'm going to get him"). Illegal possession of weapons should be presumed to indicate a threat unless careful investigation reveals otherwise (e.g., a student accidentally brought a knife to school). When in doubt about whether a student's behavior is a threat, evaluate it as a threat. (p. 1)*

All school personnel need clear and practical guidelines for identifying threats that could lead to an act of violence; remember too that threats may be made by students but also by staff members. Whenever a person verbally threatens violence or engages in behavior suggesting violence (e.g., pulling out a knife), a threat assessment must be enacted immediately to determine whether the threat is likely to be carried out.

Fein et al., (2002) include data from a joint report of the U.S. Secret Service and the U.S. Department of Education, which describe six principles for investigating potentially dangerous threats:

1. Targeted school violence can be prevented if attention is paid to early warning signs: someone who commits violence thinks about, plans, and even discusses threats with others over a period of time—they do not suddenly "snap."

2. Context is important, including both the circumstances and peer group influences on the person making the threat and the situation in which the threat is made; threatening words may actually be a bad joke or reflect a rhetorical remark, not an actual intent to commit violence.

3. Be skeptical and investigative about threats rather than jumping to conclusions based on thinking someone is "inclined to violence." There can be a tendency for some school personnel to exaggerate rumors about someone or even act on second-hand information against a student who has done nothing but is simply disliked by others.

4. Rely on facts to make your final judgment, not what you think the person "is like," as this is not profiling based on characteristics but assessment based on objective information.

5. Gather information from more than one source, including interviewing others around the person who made the threat (e.g., friends) and checking with relevant community agency personnel such as law enforcement, social workers, mental health providers, religious organizations, and others. You can do this on a confidential basis and need to do this if the threat appears to be a serious one.

6. Keep the focus on whether the student *poses a threat*, not whether the student *made a threat.* Threat assessment is all about how serious the threat is and what should be done about it, not whether the threat was made in the first place.

Having robust procedures for threat assessment is also an alternative to "zero tolerance" approaches that can lead to harsh and inappropriate punishment. There are, for example, documented cases of children expelled for doing things like bringing a toy gun to school, giving the teacher a razor blade found on the street, and having a manicure kit that included a tiny knife (Skiba & Peterson, 1999).

Cornell and Sheras (2006, p. 17) suggest the following steps for threat assessment:

Step 1: Evaluate the threat. The principal interviews the student making the threat and any witnesses, and considers context and meaning along with literal content.

Step 2: Decide whether the threat is transient or substantive. A transient threat is not serious and can easily be resolved while a *substantive* threat involves risk of potential injury to others.

Step 3: If the threat is transient, respond using disciplinary procedures (reprimand, parent notification) appropriate to the severity and chronicity of the incident.

Step 4: If the threat is substantive, is it serious or very serious? A threat to hit, assault, or beat up someone is serious, whereas a threat to kill, rape, use a weapon, or injure someone severely is very serious.

Step 5: Respond to a serious substantive threat by taking action to prevent violence, including notifying potential victims and addressing the conflict or problem associated with the threat. This completes the process for a serious substantive threat.

Step 6: Respond to a very serious substantive threat (conduct a safety evaluation) by taking immediate protective action, including contacting law enforcement, removing the student, and completing a safety evaluation, including a mental health assessment to determine referral and support needs.

Step 7: Implement a safety plan to protect potential victims and to meet the student's educational needs.

MANAGING CONFLICT AND BREAKING UP FIGHTS

At least two to three members of the senior leadership team at your school should be well trained and confident of their ability to intervene in a fight when events are out of control. As a teacher in your school, you should know who these people are and there should be discussion in a staff meeting each year about general guidelines for breaking up fights. It is a reality in today's schools that many students—even during the elementary school years—experience violence in their lives and have seen, participated in, or been the victims of a physical fight that goes beyond rough-and-tumble play. The first step in preventing violence is, of course, to avoid it. The principal and all school personnel should have basic skills and understandings of nonviolent crisis intervention, particularly nonconfrontational language that they use reliably when faced with a potentially dangerous situation or a "problem-about-to-happen." For example, a teacher may observe two students facing one another with aggressive postures, and what that teacher says can either inflame or defuse the situation. Teachers must make judgments about whether students are still in control of their own emotions or if they are so aroused that talk alone is unlikely to have the desired effect. Wolfgang (2005) describes "six steps to problem solving":

- *Step 1: Defining the problem and getting the student to acknowledge that there is a problem*
- *Step 2: Generating possible solutions and asking the student to come up with positive ways to solve the problem*
- *Step 3: Evaluating the solutions to examine the likely results of trying different approaches to solving the problem*
- *Step 4: Deciding which solution is best with the student acknowledging that decision*
- *Step 5: Implementing the (best) solution*
- *Step 6: Evaluating whether it worked for the student and solved the problem*

Teachers know that matching student violence or aggression with aggression and even shouting often just further escalates the situation. Sometimes it is better to allow a student to vent rather than demanding compliance or immediate silence. In other instances, the verbal aggression may be building towards physical attack—so good judgment is essential.

Once a teacher has determined that he or she needs to interrupt a potentially dangerous situation, how this is done is crucial. In the early phases of an aggressive incident, Wolfgang suggests that *supportive demands* can be effective rather than immediately moving to *assertive demands* which might be needed when an assault is already underway. Each approach is described next specific to situations where one or the other demand type is the better choice along with an example of how the teacher demonstrates the appropriate response.

Supportive Demands

Like adults, in certain situations students can have a "bad day" or a particularly short fuse. Some students may have ongoing anger management issues so that the teacher is already aware of risky circumstances and there may already be an intervention plan in place to deal with the student's anger. Virtually anyone can become angry when threatened or feeling attacked, either verbally or physically. One example is what often happens in busy school hallways during class changes: students can interpret that someone has deliberately pushed them aside when the behavior was not in fact intentional. Nevertheless, it can lead to conflict because it was interpreted as being on purpose. If the teacher becomes aware of a potential conflict situation before it escalates into an actual fight, carefully worded supportive demands can work well to re-capture equilibrium.

Suppose, for example, that during independent seatwork in your classroom, a student named Jack is heard talking loudly to the student Harry seated next to him, saying, *"What do you know, you're stupid! Stop looking at me, jerk!"* You can tell by looking at Jack that he is agitated—his facial expression is angry, he is leaning towards the other student in a threatening way, and he has even clenched his fists (or could be pointing at the other student). Often, the teacher will not have seen the precipitating event. This means that the first sign of trouble is already missing vital information about what led to the outburst. By definition (based on how many individuals are involved in the interaction), there are at least two versions of what happened first. In this case, the student doing the yelling has one story, and there is a second version from the student who is the recipient of the shouting. At this point, the teacher really isn't in a position to assign blame so disciplining either student will probably lead to escalation of the incident if someone feels unfairly treated. Deescalating the situation quickly is also likely to be the least disruptive to classroom activities overall, so the teacher is motivated to not lay blame and punish someone but to reestablish positive interactions and get the class back on an even keel. If the incident is symptomatic of ongoing verbal conflict between certain students, it is also important for the teacher to get to the bottom of what's happening and neutralize these interactions. Supportive demands can both deescalate impending conflict while also encouraging students to share the problem verbally and rationally rather than resorting to violence.

In this example, the teacher first moves closer to a position between the two students involved. To be prepared for such situations, the teacher might establish a place for students to sit, next to the teacher's desk, to review work that can also be used for semiprivate conversations away from the conflict area. Using supportive demands, the following is a conversation scenario:

TEACHER: [speaking in a firm but calm voice, not getting too close, and avoiding a threatening stance] "Jack, I can tell from your face that you are upset and you are angry with Harry. Could you come up by my desk with your paper and tell me about it? Harry, please keep working and after I speak with Jack, I'd like to talk with you as well."

JACK: "He's a jerk, he was laughing at me. I'm sick of it!"

[still angry and looking down rather than at the teacher]

TEACHER: "I want you to tell me what happened. But we need to go to my desk so everyone else can keep working." [don't keep talking, state this succinctly and wait for an answer]

JACK: [no answer, continues to look down]

TEACHER: "Do you want to tell me now or should we wait until later?"

JACK: "It's not my fault; I don't see why I should have to say anything."

TEACHER: "It might not be anyone's fault, it could be a misunderstanding, but I want to hear what's happening so we can solve any problems."

JACK: [doesn't say anything but moves to get up to go with the teacher to the other desk]

TEACHER: [after both are seated by the teacher's desk, looking at student at same eye level as much as possible] "I can see that you are still angry. Tell me what happened."

JACK: "I'm sick of him, he's a jerk. He thinks he's smarter than everyone else and looks down on me."

TEACHER: "Did he say something that upset you?"

JACK: "He bragged about being done already and gave me a hard time."

TEACHER: "I'll talk to Harry also, but if you yell and get angry right away when someone bothers you, how will that help?"

JACK: "I don't know!"

TEACHER: "Can you think of something else to do from the anger management strategies we talked about?"

JACK: "Yeah, I could ignore him but he just keeps at it!"

TEACHER: "I'll talk with Harry, but is there anything else you can do when someone is bothering you, if ignoring doesn't work?"

JACK: "Yeah, I know I'm supposed to see if I can get out of the situation, maybe raise my hand to get you to come over and help."

TEACHER: "That would work. You might have to keep your hand up for a count of 10 just in case I don't see you right away, alright? Now, would you go back to your seat and I'll talk to Harry about this, okay?"

JACK: "Okay" [gets up and returns to his seat with the teacher walking behind]

TEACHER: [walks back with Jack and asks Harry to join him at the teacher's desk, then goes through a similar conversation with Harry]

Assertive Demands

Wolfgang (2005) recommends using the *assertive demand* in circumstances where student behavior seems designed to elicit attention and draw others into the conflict. Assertive demands are particularly important when there is little time to lose, such as when a student's behavior has already escalated and an assault is imminent or the first blow has actually happened. Assertive demands are also needed when the student is already highly emotional and has lost control so that reasoning is unlikely to work until later, when everything is calmer. As with supportive demands, anything with the feel of "lecturing" should be avoided. These kinds of speeches by teachers (or by parents, in fact) are most often seen by young people as power plays by adults: children in the middle of a behavioral incident are not generally in a frame of mind to listen to reason and probably block out the words so that all they hear is "blah blah blah."

As with a supportive demand, the assertive demand must include both a verbal directive (the demand) and a follow-up preparatory command if the student doesn't respond to the initial directive. Suppose for example that a student named Jason is spotted by a teacher throwing stones towards a small group of three other students—not actually hitting them, but coming close enough to leave little doubt that the actions are meant to be provocative. You may also know that Jason has in the past been accused of bullying these and other students verbally and physically, so again, you are reasonably certain that the stone throwing is intentionally aimed to threaten the other students. An assertive demand sequence to intervene might be as follows:

TEACHER: [moving within five feet of the student but no closer than three feet away to give the student "personal space" and positioning self between Jason and the other students] "Jason, stop! Put the stones down now. What you are doing is dangerous and could hurt someone."

JASON: [Glaring angrily at the teacher now, continues to hold a stone tightly in each of his hands. He doesn't reply.]

TEACHER: "Jason, stop, put the stones down now!"

JASON: "Why should I? Don't tell me what to do!" [glaring and threatening gesture to throw a stone again]

TEACHER: "Put the stones down right now. If you don't, I will need to take them from you." [preparatory command, moves toward Jason]

JASON: "F—k off! No way will I put them down, they deserve it!"

TEACHER: "Stop, put the stones down or drop them on the ground." [Waits to count of 10, then grabs both Jason's arms at the wrists to prevent him throwing the stones again]

JASON: "Don't touch me! Let me go!" [attempts to pull away and then seems to try to knee the teacher in the leg, but does not make contact]

TEACHER: "I'll let go now if you drop the stones first. I'm not going to hurt you and won't let you hurt me. I will not hurt you but you must drop the stones."

JASON: "F—k off! Let me alone. You can't tell me what to do!" [still struggling, trying to pull away, and not dropping the stones]

TEACHER: "Drop the stones, I won't let go until you drop the stones. My hands are holding your wrists, but they are not hurting you. I need to keep holding you until you drop the stones and relax."

JASON: [screams several obscenities, struggles for 2 to 3 more minutes, and then suddenly drops the stones] "There! I did what you said! Now let me go!"

TEACHER: "That was the right thing to do. I'm letting go but you need to go with me to calm down and talk about what just happened." [Lets go of Jason's wrists, stands a respectful three feet away, waits for Jason to physically relax and touches his arm gently to guide him toward the building]

Note that in the example above, the teacher keeps the directives short but simple, repeating almost the exact same words until the student responds. This response is often referred to as a "broken record."

In most school environments, by the time the above scenario is unfolding, another responsible adult will have noticed and summoned further help should Jason not be responsive and/or not agree to walk back into the school with the teacher. Another student could also be asked by the teacher to get someone (who should be named) from the office or general vicinity. In this hypothetical example, Jason did respond and calmed down sufficiently for the teacher to then follow through with the appropriate consequences outlined in the school policy as well as specifically with regard to any individualized intervention plans for Jason in particular.

There will, however, also be occasions where the student does not respond and crisis intervention becomes more physical. For any situations, teachers need to feel confident that they can be firm with students in a respectful manner and not communicate fear and dislike. For some situations, however, there needs to be someone nearby or within reach quickly who is trained to intervene physically for the safety of everyone involved. This is particularly important when violence has occurred and there is serious risk to physical safety. Just as any school should have a critical mass of staff members trained in first aid, there should be a critical mass of staff trained in techniques to prevent and intervene with violence. Staff require training in how to interrupt and contravene physical assaults such as choking, biting, kicking, and hitting as well as how to use nonviolent restraint and when and how to transport a student from one location to a safer one (Wolfgang, 2005). Before help from outside the school is able to arrive, we recommend that every school has at least three different adults trained in safe physical restraint procedures to ensure that on any given day, at any given time, there is at least one person present who can be called in an emergency.

A STANDARD RESPONSE PROTOCOL (SRP) FOR SCHOOL SAFETY

Another issue important for school safety is to have in place a schoolwide, classroom response to any incident that might occur at school and place children and adults at risk. These incidents might be weather events, fires, accidental explosions, and intruders who enter the school grounds with the expressed intent of doing harm and/or to use the school as a sanctuary and those in the school as hostages. Preparing for natural disasters is fairly common in schools: Virtually all schools have regular fire drills, and schools in severe weather areas have tornado and hurricane drills. Adults who were children in school in the 1950s will even recall drills to prepare for the event of a nuclear attack, generally stooping under one's desk (hardly effective against a nuclear weapon!). The September 11, 2001, attack in New York City and various shooting incidents involving armed intruders entering school grounds with apparent indiscriminate intent to kill also raise awareness of the potential for almost "random" harm.

Given that an incident may occur with little to no advance notice, teachers need to have a plan about how to respond at the first signs of trouble—and how to signal to one another and to the children that a response is needed. Prothrow-Stith (1987) asserts that children should be taught how to keep themselves safe by learning how to prevent conflicts from escalating, how to defuse anger (their own and others'), how to recognize dangerous situations, and how to avoid weapons. Key to preparation is the establishment of a simple and effective communication system that is well understood by everyone and thus guarantees an automatic response in a crisis. Each individual teacher should have a clear policy about how to respond to different threats whether these are natural disasters, invasion by an armed intruder, or a violent outburst or suicide threat from individual students. Procedures need to be clear about what actions by teachers ensure that if there were a serious incident in their classroom, help would arrive within minutes.

Ellen Stoddard-Keyes of the National School Safety Collaborative (NS2C) has developed an umbrella program for school safety and awareness-based activities supported by the I Love U Guys Foundation (2012). As part of this program, a Standard Response Protocol (SRP) was developed as a recipe for safe schools that rehearses specific classroom responses to an incident. The SRP incorporates four specific responses to a threatening incident:

1. *Lockout:* Securing the school/building's outside perimeter

2. *Lockdown:* Securing individual rooms and keeping students quiet and in place

3. *Evacuate:* Orderly movement of students and staff from one (unsafe) location to a different (safe) location in or out of the building

4. *Shelter:* Self-protection followed by a method that has been rehearsed and may be carried out by particular designated individuals in school

SUMMARY

This chapter covers schoolwide policy and decision making by the teacher as part of transparent and fair guidelines for how the school responds to behaviors and incidents. It discusses judgments about the seriousness of behavior based on whether or not behavior causes harm or has the potential to harm others, as well as the effects on the child of the behavior being exhibited. Specific procedures are introduced that perform multiple reporting, data monitoring, and effectiveness evaluation determinations in supporting restorative school discipline. Guidelines are also included regarding intervening in conflict situations where individual students have caused harm or there is a threat to safety. The procedures described in the chapter fit within an overall preventative school ethos of Restorative School Discipline with fair and transparent consequences for identified behavior and incidents in a manner designed to ensure safety for everyone in the school environment. The final two chapters describe systems for evaluating the effectiveness of your interventions and for keeping up to date professionally with the latest developments in Restorative Classroom Discipline.

Section III

Evaluating Effectiveness and Updating Practice

9 User-Friendly Evaluation Tools and Approaches

This chapter describes tools and approaches for use by teachers and other team members to evaluate the effectiveness of interventions for individual children and schoolwide restorative practices. Individual schools may already have districtwide requirements in place to monitor student achievement, and these requirements apply to all students as well as students with behavioral challenges. In addition, there may be child development or behavioral measures used with individual children who are receiving remedial or special education services that are appropriate for other student needs. Regardless of the requirements of your school or district, teachers want to know that the time and effort they make to implement an intervention approach is time well spent. The measures included in this chapter are designed to support teacher judgments about student improvements but also to ensure that there is ample evidence to determine whether a program is working well or alternatives are needed.

MEANINGFUL OUTCOMES FOR STUDENTS AND SCHOOLS

District and school policies and practices have an effect on students, school personnel, overall school climate, the classroom, families, and the school community. Even where it is difficult to assert a causal effect, changes that parallel the implementation of particular strategies suggest a direct relationship. Of course, interventions should result in meaningful outcomes: we expect positive changes to occur when planned interventions and school activities are implemented with integrity. But sometimes when things go wrong there are also unplanned negative changes that are so closely aligned with the implementation of a new strategy that the possibility of negative side effects is a likely explanation.

The design and implementation of classroom-based and child-focused interventions and activities involve time, effort, and resources. Hence, it is important that evaluation activities are part of the planning so that teachers have confidence that their programs are resulting in intended positive outcomes and not producing unintended negative side effects. Without proper evaluation, children's precious time may be lost as already negative patterns become more entrenched and difficult to change. Furthermore, teacher time and school resources that could make a difference are wasted. It is essential to have a clear evaluation plan that doesn't have to be complicated. In this chapter, we outline a series of user-friendly tools that monitor the effectiveness of behavioral interventions (Meyer & Janney, 1992). These tools have high utility for use by busy professionals, particularly in schools and classrooms where multiple demands do not allow the kinds of clinical precision that might be reported in published literature or in a private practice with unlimited resources. The validity of user-friendly tools is established, and they can provide information that is more useful to teachers and families than even the most elegant measures accompanied by detailed reports (Meyer & Janney, 1989).

Overall Developmental Measures

The first outcome measure that should be firmly in place anytime individual children are receiving specialized services is administered at least once a year and is a measure of child development and behavior change. Whenever individualized services are provided to students on the assumption that those services have beneficial outcomes, there should be evidence reflecting that outcome. Measurement of child change over time should entail use of agreed, psychometrically validated measures for which norms exist or are being established. The comparison norms should also be appropriate for the cultural groups served by the school. Normative data tell us the level of change expected through maturation alone, so we can assess how a particular child is doing in relationship to age norms.

For students with developmental disabilities, for example, a measure such as the Scales of Independent Behavior (SIB) is very helpful as it is well-standardized internationally and includes 14 adaptive behavior scales and 8 scales representing problem behavior (Bruininks, Woodcock, Weatherman, & Hill, 1996). For students who are diagnosed with conduct disorders, measures such as the Strengths and Difficulties Questionnaire (Goodman, 1997), the Social Skills Rating System (Gresham & Elliott,

1990), and the Child Behavior Checklist (CBCL; Achenbach, 1991) are commonly used to reveal whether behavior is improving over time as a function of the intervention program. These measures require administration by someone with the appropriate qualifications such as a licensed psychologist (or mental health specialist) and services generally available depending on student referral and eligibility for special education and mental health services.

Meaningful Behavior Change

Each of the following changes in a student's behavior is important in determining whether a particular intervention is effective:

- The problem behavior improves (the challenging behavior is no longer a problem or has decreased and become more easily managed)
- Replacement skills are acquired (the student is using new skills that have been taught in situations that previously resulted in behavior problems)
- New metacognitive skills are used to manage behavior (the student has gained insight and control over his or her own behavior, predicting and preventing outbursts and other reactions by using positive thinking strategies)
- There are positive collateral effects and no negative side effects (rather than a new behavior problem occurring, the student is generally doing well and relating well with others)
- The student's placement and daily schedule is normalized (rather than requiring in-school suspension, special seating arrangements, and so forth; the student seems fine following the same routines as his or her age peers)
- Both the student and significant others are pleased with the results (whereas previously both the student and those in the environment felt stressed by interactions, there now seems to be a good fit with positive relationships developing)

We would argue that the further down the above list one goes, the more meaningful the outcomes. Thus, if the child, the family, and the teacher are pleased with how things are going, this is far more meaningful than detailed checklists or charts of the frequency or intensity of individual problem behaviors. Further, no matter what a checklist says an intervention cannot really be phased out or considered to be successful unless and until the people involved are satisfied with the outcome and the student has learned new skills and developed new, positive relationships. Similarly, if the student is still subjected to highly restrictive and controlling circumstances rather than participating fully in typical, age-appropriate activities, we don't really know if improvements in behavior have any relevance to real life.

USER-FRIENDLY DATA COLLECTION

A comprehensive and useful view of data collection for teachers goes beyond measuring problem behavior incidents. A good data system incorporates evidence of both the direct and indirect effects of interventions implemented to improve student behavior, including measurement of:

1. *New skills:* Rather than becoming angry and lashing out at others when frustrated or provoked, the student has learned how to ask for help or excuse himself or herself from uncomfortable situations in socially acceptable ways in order to recover composure.

2. *Behavior problems:* The problem behavior either isn't occurring at all or is occurring so seldom that both teachers and parents feel it is not really a problem any longer.

3. *Daily schedule and tasks:* Whereas previously the student was able to stay on task for only some of the time and tasks were modified, he or she is now able to follow the same schedule as other children in the classroom.

4. *Daily log success ratings:* As the teacher, you can report that a typical day with the student is now going well. In addition, the kinds of activities that used to provoke problem behavior no longer do, and the student is now successful on typical classroom activities and tasks working alongside others.

5. *Disciplinary actions:* School records show a decline in the number of referrals for suspensions and exclusions, and individual students who often were referred are no longer being referred.

6. *Incident records:* A comparison of office referrals and reports of incidents requiring action shows improvements both in the frequency and seriousness of challenging behavior such as aggression and disruption.

Many of the above outcomes can be monitored through data already required in schools (e.g., office referrals, suspensions, placement records, student schedules, incident records). Other data can be recorded *periodically* by a teacher rather than requiring intensive and direct behavior observation and recording, such as keeping a daily log and documenting teacher ratings of student success. Teachers are sometimes asked to keep continuous data collection records, such as checking for the presence or absence of a problem behavior every 15 minutes during selected time periods or recording frequencies across the day. While such intensive data collection systems can provide accurate information about behavior over time, it is difficult to envision how a busy regular classroom teacher with responsibility for an entire class of students can do this for one student. Consequently, such data collection systems are more likely to be found in special education classrooms or by the use of supplementary personnel such as a teacher aide (or a graduate student doing research). Even in specialist settings, however, it may not be feasible to keep accurate and reliable data on individual target behaviors without additional staff. Fortunately, the kinds of alternatives described in these handbooks fit more easily into busy schools and classrooms and can provide information that is just as useful for evaluating the effectiveness of interventions.

DATA COLLECTION FOR PROBLEM BEHAVIOR

There are various data collection approaches to monitoring instances of problem behavior that are the focus of an individualized intervention plan. Most require that a record be kept by a teacher or other staff member, but some may actually be recorded by the student. The guides highlight several approaches that demonstrate validity, are user-friendly for busy people, and which can also provide valuable information to inform the intervention plan.

Self-Monitoring

Your school consultant may recommend that the student himself or herself keep data on behaviors that are problematic. A student may, for example, keep an *anger log* to record instances where something happens that has typically resulted in problem behavior such as aggression or defiance. Self-recording contributes to the intervention by making the student more aware of the kinds of incidents that are problematic and requiring him or her to reflect on the incident as well as to report what happened next. The student typically shares the log with the school psychologist, and they work together to problem solve future situations. An additional advantage of self-recording systems such as an anger log is that the log also provides a record that can be examined for improvements over time. As part of this process, the school psychologist has a running record—at least from the student's point of view—of the student's anger management over a period of time.

Daily Log

A *daily log* can also be kept to record the student's behavior and thus provide a record of how the teacher views the behavior over the same time frame (see Figure 6). The daily log doesn't actually have to be completed every day but can be done twice weekly on a predetermined schedule such as marking in advance two random days each week on a calendar for an upcoming 4-week period (it is important to fill out the log on the agreed randomly selected dates rather than targeting "good" or "bad" days). The teacher agrees to spend 10 minutes at the end of those two days each week filling in the log. Within 3 to 4 weeks, there will be a significant amount of information about the student that not only provides evidence about whether the intervention is working, but can be used to problem solve making improvements. A daily log can also help caregivers to see patterns that might not otherwise have been noticed but are clearly having an impact on behavior—it may even reveal ways in which the mediator (teacher, teacher aide, parent) completing the log should change his or her own behavior to provide more support to the student.

Narrative daily logs such as these are actually quite good at helping caregivers learn more about the student—which is directly relevant to the student's capacity to improve. By reporting how the student does on tasks that he does or does not enjoy, patterns also emerge that can provide useful information in program planning. The teacher judgment ratings on a scale of 1 to 5 may seem arbitrary, but in fact it is the teacher's perceptions about the student that do define success of the task. Best of all, the daily log is not onerous; thus it is far more likely to actually get done in comparison to a complex, demanding data collection record.

Daily and Weekly Schedules

A weekly schedule of the student's activities in a particular class or classroom can provide a great deal of useful information if it is completed once at referral, then periodically during an intervention phase (perhaps 3 to 4 times in total across 2 to 3 months), and then again when the school psychologist feels the program has run its course. Figure 7 shows a sample schedule that the teacher completes for a given student, recording the nature of student activities and grouping arrangements along with teacher comments and a rating regarding how well things progressed. By comparing these entries for different activities and grouping configurations, it might become evident that a particular student is doing well controlling problem behavior in whole-class instruction and independent seatwork, but having difficulty in small-group work. The team working with the

Figure 6   Sample Daily Log

DAILY LOG

Student Name: _____ Day of Week/Date: _____

Log Entry By: _____

1. Overall, what kind of day did the student have? *(circle one number only)*

1	2	3	4	5
Very good day	Okay	Not sure	Not okay	Very bad day

2. How well did the student do on tasks and activities today? *(circle one number only)*

1	2	3	4	5
Very good day	Okay	Not sure	Not okay	Very bad day

3. How well did the student get on with other students today? *(circle one number only)*

1	2	3	4	5
Very well	Okay	Not sure	Not okay	Very badly

- Comment briefly on the day's events and the student's behavior. Note any incidents that occurred that seem important to you (positive and negative).
- Tasks/activities the student especially enjoyed and/or worked well on.
- Tasks/activities the student did *not* enjoy and/or work well on.

Source: Adapted from Meyer and Janney (1989).

Figure 7 Sample Student Schedule Record

Child's Weekly Schedule						
Date	**Activity**		**Time**	**Grouping**[a]	**Staff**	**Rating**[b]	**Comments**

Date	**Activity**		**Time**	**Grouping**[a]	**Staff**	**Rating**[b]	**Comments**

[a] 1:1 = One-to-one
Code: instruction
I = Independent
P = Pairs
G = Small Group
C = Whole Class

[b] + = went well, successful
Code:
V = Varied
O = Not successful

Source: Adapted from Meyer and Janney (1989).

student and the student himself or herself can then problem solve how to address remaining challenges. Again, this is the kind of data collection device that does not require an inordinate amount of time and has the advantage of providing information to monitor effects and also contribute to improving the intervention.

A successful intervention shows observable ecological and daily schedule changes that are age-appropriate. Ratings by key caregivers will also become increasingly positive. Given that these caregivers are in fact the mediators interacting with the student in the school and classroom, their satisfaction and perceptions about the student's behavior are a valid indicator of whether or not the behavior is improving.

Incident Records

Schools are required to record serious incidents whenever extreme reactive strategies are needed and used (e.g., crisis management for aggression). These incident records are intended to ensure that rights are protected and to provide evidence that the school took appropriate measures to ensure safety for everyone concerned. To evaluate the impact of policy changes, the very same *incident record* can be adapted to provide an evidence base for individual changes in student behavior as well as school rates of problem behavior across time. The sample incident record in Figure 8 does more than record what happened by requiring more detail surrounding the incident that can be used by the school principal and the team to problem solve.

An incident record such as this is completed immediately after a serious incident by the person who managed the student during the incident. It incorporates descriptive information (date/time, situation, who was present, what happened, intensity/duration, how it was managed) and reflections (why it occurred, how it might have been prevented). Reflections may not be accurate, but knowing how mediators view an incident and what they think is going on can be most helpful to intervention planning—and encouraging staff to reflect can also reveal insights and good ideas. The more generic, schoolwide incident record in Chapter 8 sits alongside the more individualized incident record represented by Figure 8. Taken together, these two records can provide the principal with valuable information and insight regarding challenges and opportunities to address those challenges.

SUMMARY

Overarching school discipline policies and practices are designed to have a positive impact on student behavior and learning. Similarly, today's

Figure 8 Sample Incident Record

Incident Record

Completed by:_____

Child's name: _____   Activity taking place: _____

Where: _____   Date/day of week: _____   Time _____

Staff present when incident occurred: _____

Children present when incident occurred: _____

1. Describe what happened just before behavior occurred. (Was the child prompted? Was a staff person attending to the child? Was the child alone? Etc.)

2. Describe what the child did and what happened through the incident. (How intense was the behavior? How long did it last? Etc.)

3. Describe what happened to the child immediately after the incident. (Include any "consequences" deliberately applied and also those that occurred without planning. Did any adults and/or children gather around? Did task demands stop? Did the adults and/or children involved get excited or stay calm? Etc.)

4. Why do you think the incident occurred?

5. How do you think the behavior could have been prevented or handled differently?

Source: Adapted from Meyer and Evans (1989).

educational systems provide intensive intervention services, supports, and programs to meet the needs of individual students with behavioral challenges. To determine whether or not these approaches are having the desired impact and effects on students and the school community, teachers need a set of evaluation measures or tools that they can actually implement in typical classrooms. In our experience, these measures can be user-friendly and, at the same time, actually provide far more useful information about how well children are doing than traditional behavioral monitoring observation systems or checklists. User-friendly measures have the added advantage of being well suited for use by busy professionals such as teachers. Many of them can also be adapted easily for use by parents and the students themselves, offering the opportunity to gain insight into behavior and thus going beyond simply monitoring behavior. The most important issue is whether data collection is done—so making it simple and useful helps to ensure that it will be done. We end our discussion of user-friendly measurement tools with a paraphrased quote that says it well:

Don't ruin good with perfect!

10 Professional Development Needs Assessment

Meaningful implementation of Restorative Classroom Discipline cannot occur unless teachers have essential knowledge, skills, and understandings about restorative practices. Each individual teacher must assume personal agency (going beyond accepting responsibility) to be professionally prepared for restorative approaches to classroom discipline and student safety. Particularly as strategies for positive approaches to behavioral challenges are continuously being updated, you'll need to assess annually whether your own knowledge, understandings, and skills about restorative practices are up to date. This chapter provides an overview of key competencies needed for Restorative Classroom Discipline and a mechanism you can use to self-assess your own professional development priorities. The chapter includes the *Professional Development Needs Assessment for Restorative Discipline* for your use in ensuring your knowledge and skills remain current.

THE NEED FOR ONGOING PROFESSIONAL DEVELOPMENT

To implement the approach described in this handbook with integrity, the teacher needs to have a strong foundation in restorative practices. Teachers may already have a great deal of knowledge about classroom management, and the vast majority of teachers are committed to supporting learning and inclusion for all students. However, in reality there is tremendous variation in the background experiences and expertise that teachers bring to the classroom. At any school, there are teachers who have been at that particular school for many years, teachers who are recently graduated and new to teaching, and experienced teachers who have come from another school or even another geographic region, including from another country.

Restorative Classroom Discipline approaches conflict in a fundamentally different way than the traditional methods derived from our legal system for dealing with serious conflict and offenses. Most adults have considerable personal experience with models of positive rewards for good behavior and retributive punishment for transgressions. For teachers, that general background in societal practices has been augmented by professional education in positive approaches to dealing with challenging behavior in the classroom. Teachers who have well-grounded pedagogical and classroom management have mastered the skill of being able to balance high academic performance expectations with a warm, positive classroom atmosphere where learning is enjoyable, students admire and look up to the teacher, and routines and rules are consistent, effective, and accepted as fair by all. However, even skillful teachers experience difficulties knowing how to manage the situation when a student doesn't respond to a classroom context that seems to be working well for nearly everyone else.

Some teachers take for granted that their students know what is expected of them in the classroom and initially may be unwilling or unable to deal with students who seem resistant to meeting those expectations. There are many different styles of teaching that work well for academic success but sometimes less well for the social-emotional development of young people. Some teachers are more directive rather than discursive in their approach to pedagogy, and these teachers may not be accustomed to involving the children themselves in emotion-related decisions such as agreeing on rules for classroom behavior. Teachers may feel it is not their job to handle students whose behavior falls outside what they consider reasonable or safe—expecting someone else such as a special education teacher, school psychologist, or the principal to solve serious behavior problems. Even today, many teachers have limited knowledge of different cultural perspectives and varied views about whether the school should fit the child or the child should fit the school. In secondary schools in particular, a proportion of the teaching staff may feel strongly that teachers are there to teach the subject and that the child's social-emotional life is not their business. Finally, teachers with the willingness in principle to be inclusive may nevertheless lack practical strategies to diffuse difficult situations in classrooms. Without professional development, they are likely to be unable to respond constructively to children who exhibit serious behavior that could put themselves and others at risk for harm. What then happens is that a teacher who is otherwise committed to supporting learning in all children may advocate instead that some children be excluded from their classroom and even from the school altogether.

It is important for you to self-assess what you know and believe about classroom and school restorative discipline, culturally responsive practices, social-emotional support, and high expectations for learning and behavior. You have information in some, but there are also areas where you have little formal training such as culturally responsive pedagogies and classroom conferencing. The principal at your school already engages in various staff appraisal activities that provide a picture of the teacher professional development needs in the school. Also, decisions are made regularly at school and at district level about professional development priorities that are addressed through special professional development (PD) initiatives and activities for teachers, and your participation in these activities may be voluntary (negotiated as part of collective bargaining), or compulsory. The PD issues identified in this chapter related to Restorative School Discipline are likely to complement or supplement ongoing PD initiatives.

THE PD NEEDS ASSESSMENT TOOL FOR RESTORATIVE DISCIPLINE

Rather than make assumptions about your knowledge and skills for restorative practices, we recommend that teachers self-assess on a regular basis to prioritize your PD needs and participation in PD activities. A sample self-report needs assessment is included here in order to help in this process of prioritizing planned professional development activities for the upcoming year and annually thereafter. The *PD Needs Assessment for Restorative Discipline* can be completed by the all-school staff, including teachers, or each teacher can elect to use it personally year by year as part of self-planning to guide teacher PD activities and opportunities. This PD needs assessment tool includes questions about all relevant components and inputs into determining priorities for PD opportunities.

One of the most valuable principles for professional learning is to continue to be a reflective teacher. In this guide, we offer a fair number of directives ourselves! There are lots of "ought," "must," and "should" demands in the text. But the ethos of restorative practices is respect for the individuals and their own strengths and goals. There is no magic formula that solves all classroom discipline concerns: something you know as well as anyone. However, the principles outlined here offer teachers a potential structure for reflection and ongoing development of newer and even better approaches in the future.

The PD Needs Assessment for Restorative Discipline

Rate your *best estimate* of the extent to which you can demonstrate each of the following:

0 = *Don't know*

1 = *None*

2 = *Some*

3 = *Most*

4 = *All*

A. Discursive and culturally responsive pedagogy and classroom management

		Don't know	None	Some	Most	All
1.	I use varied instructional approaches ranging from direct to discursive	0	1	2	3	4
2.	I establish class rules and expectations with student input	0	1	2	3	4
3.	I have knowledge of child development issues and expectations across the age range that I teach, including transition planning	0	1	2	3	4
4.	I am knowledgeable about cooperative learning and use this approach regularly	0	1	2	3	4
5.	I use systematic strategies for organizing students into small groups for in-class learning activities that are based on theories of peer relationships and support networks	0	1	2	3	4
6.	I am skillful in and regularly use classroom conferencing processes for decision making and problem solving	0	1	2	3	4

		Don't know	None	Some	Most	All
7.	I know about and use warm demander approaches to support positive behavior for learning in my classroom	0	1	2	3	4
8.	I am knowledgeable about the cultural values and mores of major cultural groups represented in my classroom and across the school	0	1	2	3	4
9.	I incorporate at least some linguistic and cultural knowledge and icons into my classroom activities for nondominant cultural student groups	0	1	2	3	4
10.	I have well-developed practices for positive and ongoing home-school communications involving my students	0	1	2	3	4
11.	I assume agency for participation in annual professional development to enhance my use of pedagogical and classroom management practices that are evidence based	0	1	2	3	4

B. Prevention of and intervention with behavior challenges

		Don't know	None	Some	Most	All
12.	I understand risks and pathways for children who exhibit behavioral challenges and/or have special needs	0	1	2	3	4
13.	I have basic skills in functional assessment to analyze children's behavioral challenges and problem solve interventions	0	1	2	3	4
14.	I appreciate that there will be different perspectives on behavior held by diverse cultures represented in the student population and school community, even if I don't know what they are	0	1	2	3	4

(Continued)

(Continued)

		Don't know	None	Some	Most	All
15.	I use available referral, support networks, and resources where appropriate to address student needs and challenges	0	1	2	3	4
16.	I have knowledge of the four major components of a positive and educative program to intervene with challenging behavior for implementation in my classroom	0	1	2	3	4
17.	I understand the important role of mediators in children's lives and can describe processes for *affective priming* to ensure that children have support to acquire new positive behaviors	0	1	2	3	4
18.	I can work collaboratively with consultant expertise to plan, implement, and evaluate an intervention for an individual student with behavioral challenges	0	1	2	3	4
19.	I can work collaboratively with other school personnel to participate actively and constructively in Restorative School Conferences to address serious behavior challenges and conflict	0	1	2	3	4
20.	I am familiar with the school's in-school suspension policy and practices and understand the process of in-school suspension reflections, including how to complete the staff reflection form	0	1	2	3	4

C. School safety and Restorative School Discipline policy

		Don't know	None	Some	Most	All
21.	I can list, define, and give examples of five key principles for restorative practices in schools—interpersonal relationships,	0	1	2	3	4

		Don't know	None	Some	Most	All
	personal dignity, mutual respect and understanding, restorative conferencing, and restitution					
22.	I am familiar with the questions for a generative restorative script in restorative conferencing	0	1	2	3	4
23.	I have knowledge of reasonable expectations for children's social-emotional capacities at different ages	0	1	2	3	4
24.	I am knowledgeable about minor and major behaviors that require an Office Discipline Referral (ODR)	0	1	2	3	4
25.	I have basic skills in threat assessment and the actions required, depending on the nature of the threat	0	1	2	3	4
26.	I can manage an assault and break up a fight either directly or by contacting the appropriate adult in the school who can intervene immediately	0	1	2	3	4
27.	I am familiar with the school's standard emergency response procedures to ensure school safety and regularly practice relevant components	0	1	2	3	4
28.	I can informally assess a suicide risk and notify the appropriate persons as needed	0	1	2	3	4
29.	I acknowledge bullying and can describe processes for addressing bullying, including seeking further advice and support to intervene	0	1	2	3	4
30.	I have knowledge of the policy and practice of Restorative School Conferencing at the school	0	1	2	3	4
31.	I have knowledge of the policy and practice of in-school suspension at the school	0	1	2	3	4

References

Achenbach, T. M. (1991). *Manual for the Child Behavior Checklist/4-18 and 1991 profile.* Burlington: University of Vermont Department of Psychiatry.

Algozzine, B., Daunic, A. P., & Smith, S.W. (2010). *Preventing problem behaviors: Schoolwide programs and classroom practices* (2nd ed.). Thousand Oaks, CA: Corwin.

Alton-Lee, A. (2003). *Quality teaching for diverse students in schooling: Best evidence synthesis.* Wellington, NZ: Ministry of Education.

American Association of Suicidology. (1998). *Suicide postvention guidelines: Suggestions for dealing with the aftermath of suicide in schools.* Washington, DC: Author. Retrieved from: http://www.suicidology.org.

American Psychological Association. (2004). Warning signs of youth violence. Retrieved from http://www.apahelpcenter.org/featuredtopics/feature.php?id=38&ch=8.

American Psychological Association Zero Tolerance Task Force. (2006). *Are zero tolerance policies effective in the schools? An evidentiary review and recommendations.* Washington, DC: Author.

Baron, M. G., Groden, J., Groden, G., & Lipsitt, L. P. (Eds.). (2006). *Stress and coping in autism.* New York, NY: Oxford University Press.

Bauer, N. S., Lozano, P., & Rivara, F. P. (2007). The effectiveness of the Olweus Bullying Prevention Program in public middle schools: A controlled trial. *Journal of Adolescent Health, 40,* 266–274.

Baumrind, D. (1991). The influence of parenting style on adolescent competence and substance use. *Journal of Early Adolescence, 11,* 56–95.

Berryman, M. (2011). The professional development process (2011). In C. E. Sleeter (Ed.), *Professional development for culturally responsive and relationship-based pedagogy* (pp. 47–67). New York, NY: Peter Lang.

Besag, V. E. (2006). *Understanding girl's friendships, fights and feuds: A practical approach to girls' bullying.* Maidenhead, UK: Open University Press.

Bierhoff, H. W., Cohen, R. L., & Greenberg, J. (Eds.). (1986). *Justice in social relations.* New York, NY: Plenum.

Bishop, R. (2011). Te Kotahitanga: Kaupapa Maori in mainstream classrooms. In C. E. Sleeter (Ed.), *Professional development for culturally responsive and relationship-based pedagogy* (pp. 23–45). New York, NY: Peter Lang.

Blake, C., Wang, W., Cartledge, G., & Gardner, R. (2000). Middle school students with serious emotional disturbances serve as social skills trainers and reinforcers for peers with SED. *Behavioral Disorders, 25,* 280–298.

Brock, S. E. (2002). School suicide postvention. In G. G. Bear, K. M. Minke, & A. Thomas (Eds.), *Children's needs II: Development, problems and alternatives* (pp. 553–576). Bethesda, MD: National Association of School Psychologists.

Brock, S.E., & Sandoval, J. (1997). Suicidal ideation and behaviors. In G.G. Bear, K.M. Minke, & A. Thomas (Eds.), *Children's needs II: Development, problems and alternatives* (pp. 361–374). Bethesda, MD: National Association of School Psychologists.

Bruininks, R. H., Woodcock, R.W., Weatherman, R. F., & Hill, B. K. (1996). *Scales of Independent Behavior-Revised (SIB-R)*. Rolling Meadows, IL: Riverside.

Bull, A., Brooking, K., & Campbell, R. (2008). *Successful home-school partnerships*. Report for the Ministry of Education, Wellington, NZ. Report available from http://www.educationcounts.govt.nz/publications.

Burns, M. K., & Gibbons, K. (2008). *Response to intervention implementation in elementary and secondary schools: Procedures to assure scientific-based practices*. New York, NY: Routledge.

Cammarota, J., & Romero, A. (2009). The Social Justice Education Project: A critically compassionate intellectualism for Chicana/o students. In W. Ayres, T. Quinn, & D. Stovall (Eds.), *Handbook for social justice education* (pp. 465–476). New York, NY: Routledge.

Campbell, A., & Anderson, C. M. (2008). Enhancing effects of check-in/check-out with function-based support. *Behavioral Disorders, 33*, 233–245.

Carr, E. G., & Durand, V. (1985).Reducing behavior problems through functional communication training. *Journal of Applied Behavior Analysis, 18*, 111–126.

Cartledge, G., & Kourea, L. (2008). Culturally responsive classrooms for culturally diverse students with and at risk for disabilities. *Exceptional Children, 74*, 351–371.

Castagno, A. E., & Brayboy, B. M. J. (2008). Culturally responsive schooling for indigenous youth: A review of the literature. *Review of Educational Research, 78*, 941–993.

Cavanagh, T. (2007).Focusing on relationships creates safety in schools. *Set: Research Information for Teachers, 1*, 31–35.

Center for Comprehensive School Reform and Improvement. (2009). *Newsletter, April 1st, 2009*. Washington, DC: Learning Point Associates. Downloaded from http://www.centerforcsri.org/files/TheCenter_NL_Apr09.pdf

Centers for Disease Control and Prevention. (2010). *Suicide: Facts at a glance*. Retrieved from http://www.cdc.gov/ViolencePrevention/pdf/Suicide_DataSheet-a.pdf.

Cheney, D., Flower, A., & Templeton, T. (2008). Applying response to intervention metrics in the social domain for students at risk of developing emotional or behavioral disorders. *The Journal of Special Education, 42*, 108–126.

Christenson, S. L., & Sheridan, S. M. (2001). *Schools and families: Creating essential connections for learning*. New York, NY: Guilford.

Cohen, J. (2006). Social, emotional, ethical, and academic education: Creating a climate for learning, participation in democracy, and well-being. *Harvard Educational Review, 76*, 201–237.

Cohen, J., McCabe, E. M., Michelli, N. M., & Pickeral, T. (2009). School climate: Research, policy, practice, and teacher education. *Teachers College Record, 111*, 180–213.

Cornell, D., & Sheras, P. (2006). *Guidelines for responding to student threats of violence*. Boston, MA: Sopris.

Covay, E., & Carbonaro, W. (2010). After the bell: Participation in extracurricular activities, classroom behavior, and academic achievement. *Sociology of Education, 83,* 20–45.

Coyne, S. M., Archer, J., & Eslea, M. (2006). "We're not friends anymore! Unless..." The frequency and harmfulness of indirect, relational, and social aggression. *Aggressive Behavior, 32,* 294–307.

Curwin, R. L., & Mendler, A. N. (1999). *Discipline with dignity.* Alexandria, VA: Association for Supervision and Curriculum Development.

Cushman, K., & Rogers, L. (2008). *Fires in the middle school bathroom: Advice for teachers from middle schoolers.* New York, NY: The New Press.

D'Augelli, A. R., Grossman, A. H., Salter, N. P., Vasey, J. J., Starks, M.T., & Sinclair, K. O. (2005). Predicting the suicide attempts of lesbian, gay, and bisexual youth. *Suicide and Life-Threatening Behavior, 35,* 646–660.

Daunic, A. P., Smith, S.W., Robinson, T. R., Miller, M. D., & Landry, K. L. (2000). Implementing schoolwide conflict resolution and peer mediation programs: Experiences in three middle schools. *Intervention in School & Clinic, 36,* 94–100.

Debski, J., Spadafore, C. D., Jacob, S., Poole, D. A., & Hixson, M. D. (2007). Suicide intervention: Training, roles, and knowledge of school psychologists. *Psychology in the Schools, 44,* 157–170.

Dunlap, G., Sailor, W., Horner, R. H., & Sugai, G. (2009). Overview and history of positive behavior support. In W. Sailor, G. Dunlap, G. Sugai, & R. Horner (Eds.), *Handbook of positive behavior support* (pp. 3–16). New York: Springer.

Evans, I. M. (1989). A multi-dimensional model for conceptualizing the design of child behavior therapy. *Behavioural Psychotherapy, 17,* 237–251.

Evans, I. M. (2010). Positive affective priming: A behavioral technique to facilitate therapeutic engagement by families, caregivers, and teachers. *Child & Family Behavior Therapy, 32,* 257–271.

Evans, I. M., Goldberg-Arnold, J. S., & Dickson, J. K. (1998). Children's perceptions of equity in peer interactions. In L. H. Meyer, H.-S. Park, M. Greno-Scheyer, I. S. Schwartz, & B. Harry (Eds.), *Making friends: The influences of culture and development* (pp. 133–147). Baltimore, MD: Paul H. Brookes.

Evans, I. M., & Harvey, S. T. (2012). *Warming the emotional climate of the primary school classroom.* Auckland, NZ: Dunmore Press.

Evans, I. M., Harvey, S. T., Buckley, L., & Yan, E. (2009). Differentiating classroom climate concepts: Academic, management, and emotional environments. *Kōtuitui: The New Zealand Journal of Social Science, 4,* 131–146.

Evans, I. M., & Meyer, L. H. (1985). *An educative approach to behavior problems: A practical decision model for interventions with severely handicapped learners.* Baltimore, MD: Paul H. Brookes.

Evans, I. M., Okifuji, A., & Thomas, A. (1995). Home-school partnerships: Involving families in the educational process. In I. M. Evans, T. Cicchelli, M. Cohen, & N. Shapiro (Eds.), *Staying in school: Partnerships for educational change* (pp. 23–40). Baltimore, MD: Paul H. Brookes.

Fein, R., Vossekuil, B., Pollack, W., Borum, R., Modzeleski, W., & Reddy, M. (2002). *Threat assessment in schools: An approach to prevent targeted violence* (NCJ 155000). Washington, DC: National Institute of Justice. Retrieved from http://www.secretservice.gov/ntac/ntac_threat.pdf.

Fergusson, D. M., Beautrais, A. L., & Horwood, L. J. (2003). Vulnerability and resiliency to suicidal behaviours in young people. *Psychological Medicine, 33,* 61–73.

Fisher, M., Bernazzani, J. P., & Meyer, L. H. (1998). Participatory action research: Supporting social relationships in the cooperative classroom. In J.W. Putnam (Ed.), *Cooperative learning and strategies for inclusion: Celebrating diversity in the classroom* (2nd ed.).(pp. 137–163). Baltimore, MD: Paul H. Brookes.

Fuchs, D., Fuchs, L. S., & Stecker, P. M. (2010). The "blurring" of special education in a new continuum of general education placements and services. *Exceptional Children, 76*, 301–323.

Garrard, W. M., & Lipsey, M. W. (2007). Conflict resolution education and antisocial behavior in U.S. schools: A meta-analysis. *Conflict Resolution Quarterly, 25*, 9–38.

Gay, G. (2010). *Culturally responsive teaching* (2nd ed.). New York: Teachers College Press.

Gazelle, H. (2006). Class climate moderates peer relations and emotional adjustment in children with an early history of anxious solitude: A child × environment model. *Developmental Psychology, 42*, 1179–1192.

Gilborn, D. (2008). Coincidence or conspiracy? Whiteness, policy and the persistence of the Black/White achievement gap. *Educational Review, 60*, 229–248.

Gladwell, M. (2008). *Outliers: The story of success.* New York: Little, Brown.

Glynn, T., Berryman, M., Bidois, P., & Atvars, K. (1997). *Bilingual behavioural checklists: Initiating a student, teacher and parent partnership in behavior management.* Unpublished paper, Poutama Pounamu Education Research Centre, Tauranga, New Zealand.

Goldstein, A. P., Glick, B., & Gibbs, J. C. (1998). *Aggression ReplacementTraining: A comprehensive intervention for aggressive youth* (rev. ed). Champaign, IL: Research Press.

Goleman, D. (1995). *Emotional intelligence: Why it can matter more than IQ.* New York, NY: Bantam.

Gonzalez, N., Moll, L. C., & Amanti, C. (2005). *Funds of knowledge: Theorizing practices in households, communities, and classrooms.* Mahwah, NJ: Lawrence Erlbaum.

Goodman, R. (1997). The Strengths and Difficulties Questionnaire: A research note. *Journal of Child Psychology and Psychiatry, 38*, 581–586.

Gottfredson, G. D., Gottfredson, D. C., & Payne, A. (2005). School climate predictors of school disorder: Results from a national study of delinquency prevention in schools. *Journal of Research in Crime and Delinquency, 42*, 412–444.

Gray, C. (1993). *The original social story book.* Jenison, MI: Jenison Public Schools.

Greene, R.W. (2008). *Lost at school: Why our kids with behavioral challenges are falling through the cracks and how we can help them.* New York, NY: Scribner.

Gresham, F. M. (2005). Response to intervention: An alternative means of identifying students as emotionally disturbed. *Education and Treatment of Children, 28*, 328–344.

Gresham, F. M., & Elliott, S. N. (1990). *Social Skills Rating System.* Circle Pines, MN: American Guidance Service.

Gutiérrez, K. D., & Rogoff, B. (2003). Cultural ways of learning: Individual traits or repertoires of practice. *Educational Researcher, 32*, 19–25.

Hamilton, M. (2008). *What's happening to our girls?* Camberwell, Victoria, Australia: Penguin Books.

Harry, B. (2008). Collaboration with culturally and linguistically diverse families: Ideal versus reality. *Exceptional Children, 74*, 372–388.

Hayes, J. M., & O'Reilly, G. (2007). *Emotional intelligence, mental health, and juvenile delinquency.* Cork, Ireland: Juvenile Mental Health Matters. Available at http://www.juvenilementalhealthmatters.com/Research_Reports_files/Mental_Health___EI_Report%5B1%5D.pdf.

Hindle, R., Savage, C., Meyer, L. H., Hynds, A., Sleeter, C.E., & Penetito, W. (2011). Culturally responsive pedagogies in the visual and performing arts: Exemplars, missed opportunities and challenges. *Curriculum Matters, 7*, 26–47.

Howlin, P., Baron-Cohen, S., & Hadwin, J. (1999). *Teaching children with autism to mind-read: A practical guide*. West Sussex, UK: Wiley.

I Love U Guys Foundation (2012). The Standard Response Protocol. Retrieved from: http://iluvuguys.org/srp.html.

Irvine, J. J. (2003). *Education teachers for diversity: Seeing with a cultural eye*. New York, NY: Teachers College Press.

Johnson, D. W, Johnson, R.T., & Holubec, E. J. (1990). *Cooperation in the classroom* (rev. ed.). Edina, MN: Interaction Books.

Juhnke, G. A., Granello, D. H., & Granello, P. F. (2011). *Suicide, self-injury, and violence in the schools: Assessment, prevention, and intervention strategies*. Hoboken, NJ: Wiley.

Kane, J., Lloyd, G., McCluskey, G., Riddell, S., Stead, J., & Weedon, E. (2007). *Restorative practices in three Scottish councils: Final report of the evaluation of the first two years of the pilot projects 2004–2006*. Edinburgh: Scottish Executive. Retrieved from www.scotland.gov.uk/Publications/2007/08/24093135.

Kendall, P. C., & Hedtke, K. A. (2006). Coping Cat workbook (2nd ed.). Philadelphia, PA: Temple University Child and Adolescent Anxiety Disorders Clinic.

Kleinfeld, J. (1975). Effective teachers of Eskimo and Indian students. *School Review, 83*, 301–344.

Kowalski, R. M., Limber, S. P., & Agatston, P. W. (2008). *Cyber bullying: Bullying in the digital age*. Malden, MA: Blackwell.

Lonner, W. J. (1980). The search for psychological universals. In H. C. Triandis & W. W. Lambert (Eds.), *Handbook of cross-cultural psychology* (Vol. 1). (pp. 143–204). Boston: Allyn and Bacon.

Lovaas, O. I. (1981). *Teaching developmentally disabled children: The ME book*. Baltimore, MD: University Park Press.

Maccoby, E. E., & Martin, J. A. (1983). Socialization in the context of the family: Parent–child interaction. In P. Mussen & E. M. Hetherington (Eds.), *Handbook of child psychology, Vol. IV: Socialization, personality, and social development* (4th ed.). (pp. 1–101). New York, NY: Wiley.

McCluskey, G., Lloyd, G., Kane, J., Riddell, S., Stead, J., & Weedon, E. (2008). Can restorative practices in schools make a difference? *Educational Review, 60*, 405–417.

McGee, J. J., Menolascino, F. J., Hobbs, D. C., & Menousek, P. E. (1987). *Gentle teaching: A non-aversive approach to helping persons with mental retardation*. New York: Human Sciences Press.

McIntosh, K., Campbell, A. L., Carter, D. R., & Zumbo, B. D. (2009). Concurrent validity of office discipline referrals and cut points used in schoolwide positive behavior support. *Behavioral Disorders, 34*, 100–113.

Meyer, L. H., & Evans, I. M. (1989). *Nonaversive intervention for behavior problems: A manual for home and community*. Baltimore, MD: Paul H. Brookes.

Meyer, L. H., & Fisher, M. (1999). Participatory research on strategies to support inclusion. *Set Special 1999: Special Education, 5*, 1–4.

Meyer, L. H., & Henry, L. A. (1993). Cooperative classroom management: Student needs and fairness in the regular classroom. In J.W. Putnam (Ed.), *Cooperative learning and strategies for inclusion: Celebrating diversity in the classroom* (pp. 93–121). Baltimore, MD: Paul H. Brookes.

Meyer, L. H., & Janney, R. E. (1989). User-friendly measures of meaningful outcomes: Evaluating behavioural interventions. *Journal of The Association for Persons with Severe Handicaps, 14,* 263–270.

Meyer, L. H., & Janney, R. E. (1992). School-based consultation to support students with severe behavior problems in integrated educational programs. In T. Kratochwill, S. Elliott, & M. Gettinger (Eds.), *Advances in School Psychology* (Vol. 8). (pp. 153–193). Hillsdale, NJ: Lawrence Erlbaum.

Minke, K. M., & Anderson, K. J. (2005). Family-school collaboration and positive behavior support. *Journal of Positive Behavior Interventions, 7,* 181–185.

Molloy, P., Fleming, G., Rodriguez, X. R., Saavedra, N., Tucker, B., & Williams, D. L. Jr. (1995). *Building home, school, community partnerships: The planning phase.* Austin, TX: Southwest Educational Development Laboratory.

National Juvenile Justice Network (2007). *Fact sheet: Youth who commit sexual offences.* Washington, DC: Author.

Nickerson, A. B., & Zhe, E. J. (2004). Crisis prevention and intervention: A survey of school psychologists. *Psychology in the Schools, 41,* 777–788.

Olweus, D. (2003). A profile of bullying at school. *Educational Leadership, 60*(6), 12–17.

Paley, V. (1992). *You can't say you can't play.* Cambridge, MA: Harvard University Press.

Poland, S., & McCormick, J. S. (1999). *Coping with crisis: Lessons learned.* Longmont, CO: Sopris West.

Prothrow-Stith, D. (1987). *Violence prevention curriculum for adolescents.* Newton, MA: Education Development Center.

Putnam, J. W. (1998). The process of cooperative learning. In J.W. Putnam (Ed.), *Cooperative learning and strategies for inclusion: Celebrating diversity in the classroom* (2nd ed.).(pp. 17–47). Baltimore, MD: Paul H. Brookes.

Robinson, T. R., Smith, S. W., & Daunic, A. P. (2000). Middle school students' views on the social validity of peer mediation. *Middle School Journal, 31,* 23–29.

Roseth, C. J., Johnson, D. W., & Johnson, R. T. (2008).Promoting early adolescents' achievement and peer relationships: The effects of cooperative, competitive, and individualistic goal structures, *Psychological Bulletin, 134,* 223–246.

Ross, D. D., Bondy, E., Gallingane, C., & Hambacher, E. (2008). Promoting academic engagement through insistence: Being a warm demander. *Childhood Education, 84,* 142–146.

Salisbury, C. L., Evans, I. M., & Palombaro, M. M. (1997). Collaborative problem-solving to promote the inclusion of young children with significant disabilities in primary grades. *Exceptional Children, 63,* 195–209.

Sapon-Shevin, M., Dobbelaere, A., Corrigan, C. R., Goodman, K., & Mastin, M.C. (1998). Promoting inclusive behavior in inclusive classrooms: "You can't say you can't play". In L. H. Meyer, H.-S. Park, M. Grenot-Scheyer, I. S. Schwartz, & B. Harry (Eds.), *Making friends: The influences of culture and development* (pp. 105–132). Baltimore, MD: Paul H. Brookes.

Savage, C. (2009). Culturally responsive behavior management. In V. Green & S. Cherrington (Eds.), *Delving into diversity: An international exploration of diversity in education* (pp. 35–44). New York, NY: Nova.

Savage, C., Lewis, J., & Colless, N. (2011). Essentials for implementation: Six years of schoolwide positive behavior support in NZ. *New Zealand Journal of Psychology, 40*(1), 29–37.

Schindler, H. R., & Horner, R. H. (2005). Generalized reduction of problem behavior of young children with autism: Building trans-situational interventions. *American Journal on Mental Retardation, 110*, 36–47.

Shields, C., Bishop, R., & Mazawi, A. (2005). *Pathologizing practices: The impact of deficit thinking on education.* New York, NY: Peter Lang.

Skiba, R. J., & Peterson, R. L. (1999). The dark side of zero tolerance: Can punishment lead to safe schools? *Phi Delta Kappan, 80*, 372–382.

Skiba, R. J., Simmons, A. B., Ritter, S., Gibbs, A. C., Rausch, M. K., Cuadrado, J., & Chung, C.-G. (2008). Achieving equity in special education: History, status, and current challenges. *Exceptional Children, 74*, 264–288.

Sleeter, C. S. (2011). (Ed.). *Professional development for culturally responsive and relationship-based pedagogy.* New York, NY: Peter Lang.

Sleeter, C. E., & Grant, C. A. (2009). *Making choices for multicultural education: Five approaches to race, class, and gender* (6th ed.). Hoboken, NJ: Wiley.

Somersalo, H., Solantaus, T., & Almqvist, F. (2002). Classroom climate and the mental health of primary school children. *Nordic Journal of Psychiatry, 56*, 285–290.

Strong, K., & Cornell, D. (2008). Student threat assessment in Memphis City schools: A descriptive report. *Behavioral Disorders, 34*, 42–54.

Sue, S. (1998). In search of cultural competence in psychotherapy and counseling. *American Psychologist, 53*, 440–448.

Sugai, G., Horner, R., Sailor, W., Dunlap, G., Eber, L., Lewis, T., . . . Nelson, M. (2005). *School-wide positive behavior support: Implementers' blueprint and self-assessment.* Washington, DC: Technical Assistance Center on Positive Behavioral Interventions and Supports.

Todd, A. W., Horner, R., & Dickey, C. R. (2010, August). SWIS Documentation Project Referral Form Examples, Version 4.4. Retrieved from http://www.swis.org/index.php?page=resources;rid=1025-.

Varnham, S. (2008). Keeping them connected: Restorative justice in schools in Australia and New Zealand—what progress? *Australia & New Zealand Journal of Law & Education, 13*, 71–82.

Valenzuela, A. (1999). *Subtractive schooling: U.S. Mexican youth and the politics of caring.* Albany, NY: State University of New York Press.

Vincent, C. G., & Tobin, T. J. (2011). The relationship between implementation of school-wide positive behaviour support (SWPBS) and disciplinary exclusion of students from various ethnic backgrounds with and without disabilities. *Journal of Emotional and Behavioral Disorders, 19*, 217–232.

Walker, H. M., Horner, R. H., Sugai, G., Bullis, M., Sprague, J. R., Bricker, D., & Kaufman, M.J. (1996). Integrated approaches to preventing antisocial behavior patterns among school-age children and youth. *Journal of Emotional and Behavioral Disorders, 4*, 194–209.

Wanzek, J., & Vaughn, S. (2009). Students demonstrating persistent low response to reading intervention: Three case studies. *Learning Disabilities Research and Practice, 24*, 151–163.

Ware, F. (2006). Warm demander pedagogy: Culturally responsive teaching that supports a culture of achievement for African American students. *Urban Education, 41,* 427–456.

Wolfgang, C. H. (2005). *Solving discipline and classroom management problems: Methods and models for today's teachers* (6th ed.). Hoboken, NJ: Wiley.

Wubbels, T., & Brekelmans, M. (2005). Two decades of research on teacher-student relationships in class. *International Journal of Educational Research, 43,* 6–24.

Zehr, H. (1990). *Changing lenses.* Scottdale, PA: Herald Press.

Zehr, H. (2002). *The little book of restorative justice.* Intercourse, PA: Good Books.

Zimring, F. E. (2004). *An American travesty: Legal responses to adolescent sexual offending.* Chicago, IL: University of Chicago Press.

Index

Abbas (case study), 42–43
Achenbach, T. M., 165
Aesthetic caring, 51
African American teachers, 51–52
Agatston, P. W., 69
Aggression Replacement Training
(ART), 117
Aggressive behaviors, 149–152
Algozzine, B., 78
Almqvist, F., 39
Alton-Lee, A., 50
Always learning behaviors, 14–16
Amanti, C., 52–53
American Association of Suicidology,
143, 146
American Psychological Association, 144
American Psychological Association
Zero Tolerance Task Force, 86
Amish school incident, 149
Anderson, C. M., 9
Anderson, K. J., 29
Antecedents, behaviors, and consequences
(ABC) analysis, 100–101
Antecedent settings and events, 100–102
Anti-bullying strategies, 72–73
Archer, J., 70
Assertive demands, 155–157
Atvars, K., 24
Authentic caring, 51–52
Authoritarian parenting, 49
Authoritative parenting, 49
Autistic spectrum disorders (ASD), 113

Baron-Cohen, S., 113
Baron, M. G., 114
Barriers to change, 90
Bauer, N. S., 72
Baumrind, D., 48
Beautrais, A. L., 144

Behavior change measures, 165–166
Behavior expectations
classroom rules, 17–21
clearly stated rules, 13–14
cultural mismatches, 26–27
home-school partnerships, 29–31
individualized intervention strategies,
83–98
judgment-based assessments, 125–128
schoolwide behavioral expectations,
14–16, 125–128
seriousness indicators, 125–127
teachers' role, 16–17
Bernazzani, J. P., 60
Berryman, M., 24, 54
Besag, V. E., 71
Bidois, P., 24
Bierhoff, H. W., 65
Bishop, R., 26, 27, 33, 50, 51, 53
Blake, C., 78
Bondy, E., 51
Borum, R.
see Fein, R.
Brayboy, B. M. J., 50
Breaking up fights, 151–157
Brekelmans, M., 48, 49
Bricker, D.
see Walker, H. M.
Brock, S. E., 145, 147
Brooking, K., 28
Bruininks, R. H., 164
Buckley, L., 40
Bull, A., 28
Bullis, M.
see Walker, H. M.
Bullying
cyberbullying, 70–71
identification strategies, 70
impacts, 69

prevention and intervention strategies, 72–73
schoolwide behavioral expectations, 16
Burns, M. K., 85

Cammarota, J., 53
Campbell, A., 9
Campbell, A. L., 128
Campbell, R., 28
Carbonaro, W., 56
Caring behaviors, 14–16
Carr, E. G., 112
Carter, D. R., 128
Cartledge, G., 26, 78
Case studies
   Abbas, 42–43
   Dilbert, 115–118
   Fernanda, 118–123
   Jayla, 87–90, 102, 105, 108, 109–110
   Justin, 110–115
   Nikotemo, 91–92, 101, 104–105, 108
   Samuel, 103–104, 107
   third-grade classroom disruption, 46
Castagno, A. E., 50
Cavanagh, T., 74
CBT Workbook for Children & Adolescents
   (O'Reilly), 123
Cell phones, 70
Center for Comprehensive School Reform
   and Improvement, 39–40
Centers for Disease Control and
   Prevention, 143, 144
Cheney, D., 84
Child Behavior Checklist (CBCL), 165
Child-focused planning, 83–98
   see also Intervention strategies
Christenson, S. L., 29
Chung, C.-G.
   see Skiba, R. J.
Classroom climate
   characteristics, 6–7
   cultural responsiveness, 50–54
   elementary classrooms, 44–46
   implementation strategies, 37–38
   school climate, 46–48
   secondary classrooms, 41–43
   socioemotional development, 55–57
Classroom environments, 7
Classroom ethos, 8–9
Cognitive behavior therapy (CBT),
   109, 123
Cognitive distortions, 109–110
Cohen, J., 6, 47
Cohen, R. L., 65

Collaborative problem solving strategies,
   65–69
Colless, N., 8, 133
Columbine High School (Colorado), 149
Communication strategies, 32–34
Community relationships
   see Home-school relationships
Conflict management, 73–76, 151–157
Conflict Resolution Education (CRE), 72
Consequences, 106–108, 114
Consultant services, 126
Contagion suicide, 145
Cooperative learning structures, 56–59
Coping Cat©, 106
Coping strategies, 105–106
Copycat suicide, 145
Cornell, D., 128, 149, 151
Corrigan, C. R., 19–21
Covay, E., 56
Coyne, S. M., 70
CRC technique (commend, recommend,
   and commend again), 42
Creating a Positive School Climate for
   Learning toolkit, 47–48
Cuadrado, J.
   see Skiba, R. J.
Culturally and linguistically diverse
   (CLD) students, 25–28
Culturally competent teachers, 27–28,
   42, 91–92
Cultural responsiveness
   authentic caring, 51–52
   classroom climate, 50–51
   culturally responsive pedagogies, 52–54
   restorative practices, 91–92
Curwin, R. L., 85
Cushman, K., 41
Cyberbullying, 70–71

Daily logs, 168, 169
Daily schedules, 168, 170, 171
Data collection
   problem behavior, 167–171
   user-friendly data collection, 166–167
D'Augelli, A. R., 144
Daunic, A. P., 72, 78
Debski, J., 144, 147
Deficit theory perspective, 27, 87–90
Developmental measures, 164–165
Dialectical behavior therapy (DBT), 120
Dickey, C. R., 131
Dickson, J. K., 66
Digital media, 42
Dilbert (case study), 115–118

Dimensional model of interpersonal teacher behavior, 48–50
Discussion paper, 10–11
Disproportionate suspensions, 39–40
Dobbelaere, A., 19–21
Dominant culture, 50–51
Dunlap, G., 8
Durand, V., 112

Eber, L.
  see Sugai, G.
Ecological change, 100–101
Ed Smith Elementary School, 19–21
Educative principles, 8–9
Effective teaching profile (ETP), 53–54
Effort to Implement Scale, 96
Elementary classrooms, 44–46
Elliott, S. N., 164
Emergency response plans, 157–158
Emotional competence, 38–40, 44–45
Emotional distortions, 109–110
Emotional intelligence, 38
Emotion management skills, 45
Empathy, 38
Environmental triggers, 100–101
Eslea, M., 70
Evaluation tools
  data collection, 166–171
  meaningful outcomes, 163–166
  usefulness, 173
Evans, I. M., 8, 31, 40, 44, 66–67, 73, 93, 97, 110, 172

Face-to-face interaction, 57
Facilitators, 134–135
Fairness, 65–67, 126–127
Fein, R., 150
Fergusson, D. M., 144
Fernanda (case study), 118–123
Fights, 151–157
Fisher, M., 60, 62, 64
Fleming, G., 29
Flower, A., 84
Four-component intervention model, 97–98
Fuchs, D., 84, 85
Fuchs, L. S., 84, 85

Gallingane, C., 51
Gardner, R., 78
Garrard, W. M., 72
Gay, G., 28, 52, 53
Gazelle, H., 39
Gentle teaching approach, 112
Gibbons, K., 85

Gibbs, A. C.
  see Skiba, R. J.
Gibbs, J. C., 117
Gilborn, D., 51
Gladwell, M., 90
Glick, B., 117
Glynn, T., 24, 28
Goal setting, 58
Goldberg-Arnold, J. S., 66
Goldstein, A. P., 117
Goleman, D., 38
Gonzalez, N., 52–53
Goodman, K., 19–21
Goodman, R., 164
Gottfredson, D. C., 39
Gottfredson, G. D., 39
Granello, D. H., 145
Granello, P. F., 145
Grant, C. A., 28, 50
Gray, C., 112
Greenberg, J., 65
Greene, R. W., 88, 89, 101, 108–109
Gresham, F. M., 85, 164
Groden, G., 114
Groden, J., 114
Grossman, A. H.
  see D'Augelli, A. R.
Group problem solving processes, 65–69
Gutiérrez, K. D., 50

Hadwin, J., 113
Hambacher, E., 51
Hamilton, M., 71
Harry, B., 26, 28
Harvey, S. T., 40, 44, 73, 110
Hayes, J. M., 123
Hedtke, K. A., 106
Henry, L. A., 60, 61
Heterogeneous groups, 58
Hill, B. K., 164
Hindle, R., 54, 70
Hixson, M. D.
  see Debski, J.
Hobbs, D. C., 112
Holubec, E. J., 57
Home-school relationships
  communication strategies, 32–34
  culturally and linguistically diverse (CLD) students, 25–28
  cultural mismatches, 26–27
  home-school partnerships, 28–34
  in-school suspension, 139, 140
  parent-teacher interactions, 23–25
  problem contexts and behaviors, 24–25

Horner, R. H., 8, 96, 131
   see also Walker, H. M.
Horwood, L. J., 144
Hostile intent, 109, 126–127
Howlin, P., 113
Humor, 70
Hynds, A., 54, 70

I Love U Guys Foundation, 158
Incident records, 171, 172
Incident reports, 128–133
Individual accountability, 57
Individualized educational plans
   (IEPs), 28
Individualized intervention strategies,
   83–98
Individuals with Disabilities Education
   Improvement Act (IDEIA), 81, 84
In-school suspension, 135–142
Internet, 42
Interpersonal relationships, 73–74
Intervention strategies
   barriers to change, 90
   culturally responsive practices, 91–92
   deficit thinking, 87–90
   four-component intervention model,
      97–98
   general principles, 86–96
   individual students, 83–98
   mediation strategies, 93–96
   PERT (prevent, educate, restore, think)
      model, 97–124
   secondary and tertiary prevention and
      intervention, 84–86
Irvine, J. J., 51

Jacob, S.
   see Debski, J.
Janney, R. E., 164, 169, 170
Jarrett Middle School (Hawai'i), 14–16, 17
Jayla (case study), 87–90, 102, 105,
   108, 109–110
Johnson, D. W., 57, 58
Johnson, R. T., 57, 58
Judgment-based assessments, 125–127
Juhnke, G. A., 145
Justin (case study), 110–115

Kane, J., 77
   see also McCluskey, G.
Kaufman, M.J.
   see Walker, H. M.
Kendall, P. C., 106
Kleinfeld, J., 48, 51

Kourea, L., 26
Kowalski, R. M., 69

Landry, K. L., 72
Learning outcomes, 2
Level 1 interventions, 84–85
Level 2 interventions, 85
Level 3 interventions, 85
Lewis, J., 8, 133
Lewis, T.
   see Sugai, G.
Limber, S. P., 69
Lipsey, M. W., 72
Lipsitt, L. P, 114
Lloyd, G., 77
   see also McCluskey, G.
Lonner, W. J., 48
Lovaas, O. I., 111
Lozano, P., 72

Maccoby, E. E., 49
Major versus minor behavior problems,
   131–132
Maori students, 28, 53
Martin, J. A., 49
Mastin, M.C., 19–21
Mazawi, A., 26
McCabe, E. M., 6
McCluskey, G., 5, 11, 77
McCormick, J. S., 146
McGee, J. J., 112
McIntosh, K., 128
Meaningful behavior change measures,
   165–166
Meaningful outcomes measures, 163–166
Mediation strategies
   Effort to Implement Scale, 96
   mediators, 93–96
   restorative practices, 76–78
Mendler, A. N., 85
Menolascino, F. J., 112
Menousek, P. E., 112
Mentoring programs, 78–79
Meta-emotion, 44–45
Meyer, L. H., 8, 54, 60, 61, 62, 64, 70, 97,
   164, 169, 170, 172
Michelli, N. M., 6
Miller, M. D., 72
Minke, K. M., 29
Minneapolis Public School system, 47–48
Minoritized cultures, 26–27
Modzeleski, W.
   see Fein, R.
Moll, L. C., 52–53

Molloy, P., 29
Mood management, 38
Motivational interviewing, 120
Mutual respect and understanding, 74

National Association of School
    Psychologists (NASP), 143
National Juvenile Justice Network, 116
National School Climate Center
    (NSCC), 47
National School Safety Collaborative
    (NS2C), 158
Natural consequences, 106–107, 114
Negative conversations, 88–89
Nelson, M.
    see Sugai, G.
New Zealand, 28, 53, 133
Nickerson, A. B., 143
Nikotemo (case study), 91–92, 101,
    104–105, 108

Objective documentation, 128–133
Office Discipline Referrals (ODR), 128–133
Okifuji, A., 31
Olweus Bullying Prevention Program,
    72–73
Olweus, D., 72
O'Reilly, G., 123
Outliers: The Story of Success (Gladwell), 90

Paeroa College, 142
Paley, V., 18–19
Palombaro, M. M., 66–67
Parental involvement, 28–34
Parenting styles, 49
Payne, A., 39
Pedagogy
    classroom climate, 7, 40
    culturally responsive pedagogies, 52–54
Peer mediation, 77, 77–78
Peer support networks, 55–56, 59–64
Penetito, W., 54, 70
Permissive parenting, 49
Personal dignity, 74
PERT (prevent, educate, restore, think)
    model
    characteristics, 97–98, 99
    Dilbert (case study), 115–118
    educate component, 102–106
    Fernanda (case study), 118–123
    Justin (case study), 110–115
    plan summary, 124
    prevent component, 100–102
    replacement skills, 102–106

restore component, 106–108
think component, 108–110
Peterson, R. L., 151
Pickeral, T., 6
Poland, S., 146
Pollack, W.
    see Fein, R.
Poole, D. A.
    see Debski, J.
Positive affective priming, 93–94
Positive behavior management, 8
Positive interdependence, 57
Precipitating events, 100–101
Problem-solving strategies, 65–69, 152
Professional development
    importance, 175–177
    needs assessment tool, 177–181
Prosocial behavior, 38
Prothrow-Stith, D., 158
Punishment approaches, 8, 126–127
Putnam, J. W., 57

Rausch, M. K.
    see Skiba, R. J.
Reddy, M.
    see Fein, R.
Red Lake High School (Minnesota), 149
Reflective activities, 139, 141–142
Reinforcement versus replacement,
    103–104
Relational aggression, 70–71
Relationships
    classroom climate, 7
    emotional competence, 38
Replacement skills, 102–106
Respect, 74
Response to Intervention (RTI)
    model, 85
Responsible behaviors, 14–16
Restitution, 74
Restorative classroom discipline
    classroom climate, 6–7
    classroom ethos, 8–9
    home-school relationships, 23–25
    implementation strategies, 10–11
    individualized intervention strategies,
        83–98
    key characteristics, 5–6
    mediation strategies, 76–78
    PERT (prevent, educate, restore, think)
        model, 97–124
    planning guidelines, 7–11
    prevention and intervention strategies,
        9–10

professional development needs,
175–181
restorative conferences, 74, 79–80
restorative curricula, 73–76
structures and processes, 73–79
see also Classroom climate
Restorative conferences, 74, 79–80, 133–135
Restorative justice, 73
Restorative language and conversations,
73–76
Retribution approaches, 8, 126–127
Riddell, S., 77
see also McCluskey, G.
Risky behaviors, 41–42
Ritter, S.
see Skiba, R. J.
Rivara, F. P., 72
Robinson, T. R., 72, 78
Rodriguez, X. R., 29
Rogers, L., 41
Rogoff, B., 50
Romero, A., 53
Roseth, C. J., 57, 58
Ross, D. D., 51

Saavedra, N., 29
Safety considerations, 6–7, 41–42, 107–108
Sailor, W., 8
Salisbury, C. L., 66–67
Salter, N. P.
see D'Augelli, A. R.
Samuel (case study), 103–104, 107
Sandoval, J., 145
Sapon-Shevin, M., 19–21
Savage, C. M., 8, 28, 54, 70, 133
Scales of Independent Behavior (SIB), 164
Schindler, H. R., 96
School climate, 46–48
Schoolwide behavioral expectations
Jarrett Middle School (Hawai'i), 14–16
judgment-based assessments, 125–128
Office Discipline Referrals (ODR),
128–133
restorative conferences, 133–135
Schoolwide Positive Behavior Support
(SWPBS), 127, 133
Seating arrangements, 56, 59–63
Secondary classrooms, 41–43
Secondary intervention programs, 9
Secondary prevention and intervention,
84–86
Self-awareness, 38
Self-monitoring processes, 167–171

Self-motivation, 38
Self-regulation, 45
Sense of belonging, 39–40
Sense of humor, 70
Setting events, 100–101
Sexual offending, 116
Sheras, P., 149, 151
Sheridan, S. M., 29
Shields, C., 26
Shuttle mediation, 78
Simmons, A. B.
see Skiba, R. J.
Sinclair, K. O.
see D'Augelli, A. R.
Skiba, R. J., 26, 151
Sleeter, C. E., 28, 33, 50, 53, 54, 70
Smith, S. W., 72, 78
Social justice, 65–67
Social media, 42
Social Skills Rating System, 164
Social stories, 112–113
Socioemotional development, 55–57
Solantaus, T., 39
Somersalo, H., 39
Spadafore, C. D.
see Debski, J.
Special education services, 84–85
Sprague, J. R.
see Walker, H. M.
Standard Emergency Response Protocol
(SERP), 157–158
Standard Response Protocol (SRP), 158
Starks, M.T.
see D'Augelli, A. R.
Stead, J., 77
see also McCluskey, G.
Stecker, P. M., 84, 85
Stoddard-Keyes, E., 158
Strengths and Difficulties
Questionnaire, 164
Stress management strategies, 113–114
Strong, K., 128, 149
Structured cooperative learning
groups, 56–59
Student Interest Inventory, 60, 62
Student pairs and groups, 59–64
Student reflection, 58
Student suicide, 143
Student-teacher interactions
elementary classrooms, 44–46
in-school suspension, 139, 140
secondary classrooms, 41–43
Sue, S., 27

Sugai, G., 8, 127
   see also Walker, H. M.
Suicide prevention and intervention
   communication strategies, 145–147
   risk factors, 143–145
   school response, 145–147
   student suicides, 143
   teacher self-assessment, 147–148
   warning signs, 144–145
Supportive demands, 153–155
Support structures
   community support, 55–56
   cooperative learning structures, 56–59
   peer support networks, 55–56, 59–64
Suspension, 135–142
Syracuse, New York, 18–19

Teachable moments, 42, 45
Teacher-student interactions
   elementary classrooms, 44–46
   in-school suspension, 139, 140
   secondary classrooms, 41–43
Teaching styles
   African American teachers, 51–52
   characteristics, 48–50
Teasing, 70
Te Kotahitanga teacher professional
   development program, 53
Templeton, T., 84
Tertiary intervention programs, 9–10
Tertiary prevention and intervention,
   84–86
Text messages, 70
Third-grade classroom disruption case
   study, 46
Thomas, A., 31
Threat assessment, 128, 149–151
Threatening behaviors, 41–42
Tier 1 interventions, 9
Tier 2 interventions, 9
Tier 3 inverventions, 9–10
Tobin, T. J., 26, 136
Todd, A. W., 131
Transparency, 126–127
Trigger events, 100–101

Tucker, B., 29
Tucson, Arizona, 53

Umbria, A., 64
Unfairness, 65–67, 126–127
Uninvolved parenting, 49
Universal interventions, 84
U.S. Department of Education, 150
U.S. Secret Service, 149, 150

Valenzuela, A., 51
Varnham, S., 11, 80
Vasey, J. J.
   see D'Augelli, A. R.
Vaughn, S., 85
Vincent, C. G., 26, 136
Violence prevention
   see Fights; Threat assessment
Virginia Tech University, 149
Vossekuil, B.
   see Fein, R.

Walker, H. M., 10, 84
Wang, W., 78
Wanzek, J., 85
Ware, F., 51–52
Weatherman, R. F., 164
Weedon, E., 77
   see also McCluskey, G.
Weekly schedules, 168, 170, 171
Williams, D. L., Jr., 29
Winkler, N., 64
Wolfgang, C. H., 152, 155, 157
Woodcock, R.W., 164
Wubbels, T., 48, 49

Yan, E., 40
YCSYCP rule, 19–21
You Can't Say You Can't Play (Paley), 18–19

Zehr, H., 10, 11, 73
Zero-tolerance policies, 86
Zhe, E. J., 143
Zimring, F. E., 116
Zumbo, B. D., 128

CORWIN

A SAGE Company

The Corwin logo—a raven striding across an open book—represents the union of courage and learning. Corwin is committed to improving education for all learners by publishing books and other professional development resources for those serving the field of PreK–12 education. By providing practical, hands-on materials, Corwin continues to carry out the promise of its motto: **"Helping Educators Do Their Work Better."**